The CALVIN INSTITUTE OF CHRISTIAN WORSHIP LITURGICAL STUDIES Series, edited by John D. Witvliet, is designed to promote reflection on the history, theology, and practice of Christian worship and to stimulate worship renewal in Christian congregations. Contributions include writings by pastoral worship leaders from a wide range of communities and scholars from a wide range of disciplines. The ultimate goal of these contributions is to nurture worship practices that are spiritually vital and theologically rooted.

PUBLISHED

Singing God's Psalms

Metrical Psalms and Reflections
for Each Sunday in the Church Year

Fred R. Anderson

WILLIAM B. EERDMANS PUBLISHING COMPANY

GRAND RAPIDS, MICHIGAN

Wm. B. Eerdmans Publishing Co.
2140 Oak Industrial Drive NE, Grand Rapids, Michigan 49505
www.eerdmans.com

Published 2016
Printed in the United States of America

22 21 20 19 18 17 16   1 2 3 4 5 6 7

ISBN 978-0-8028-7321-7

Library of Congress Cataloging-in-Publication Data

Names: Anderson, Fred R., author.
Title: Singing God's Psalms : metrical Psalms and reflections for each Sunday in the
    church year / Fred R. Anderson.
Description: Grand Rapids : Eerdmans Publishing Co., 2016. |
    Series: The Calvin Institute of Christian Worship liturgical studies series
Identifiers: LCCN 2016030247 | ISBN 9780802873217 (pbk. : alk. paper)
Subjects: LCSH: Bible. Psalms — Paraphrases, English. | Psalmody. |
    Bible. Psalms — Meditations. | Common lectionary (1992)
Classification: LCC BS1440 .A53 2016 | DDC 264/.15 — dc23
    LC record available at https://lccn.loc.gov/2016030247

Contents

Foreword

We keep returning to the Psalms because they constitute our most durable and reliable script for utterance of the fullness of our life to God. Their clear but fluid genres allow ample room for adaptation to specific circumstance while still providing structure and constancy to the deepness of our emotional life. The playfulness of image and metaphor permit these poems to be wondrously and teasingly contemporary.

And of course they are to be sung! The Common Lectionary assures that the Psalms will remain available in the life and worship of the church. The lectionary pattern of the Psalms, moreover, is increasingly used in "non-liturgical" churches as well as more traditionally in "liturgical churches." But of course, if they are to be sung, we need a good match between the words given us and the music through which they are rendered. Fred Anderson now has provided us with a casting of the words of the Psalter in metrical cadences that permit versification and dynamic moment through the journey of the Psalms. To make them "metric" requires that they be translated so that a certain cadence will correspond to the rhythm and beat of already existing music. He has, moreover, connected the Psalms to a large inventory of familiar hymns. As a prodigious accomplishment he has included metric psalm-cum-music for every Sunday in the three-year cycle of the lectionary. His work evidences a keen ear for nuance so that the match of words and music is not happenstance, but is done with sensitivity to the faith being articulated. This is indeed a major artistic achievement and a major gift to the church. Church musicians are always seeking fresh ways to render familiar texts, and Anderson now has responded to that need in a compelling and sensitive way.

Of course it is most unfortunate that such a sequence as the lectionary provides leaves out many poignant psalms, notably laments and complaints. That of course is no failure on Anderson's part; rather, it reflects the timidity and cowardice of a lectionary that seeks to protect us from the less "friendly" aspects of the Psalter. One may hope for a much-needed revision of the lectionary in this regard so that more such psalms could be included; that would send Anderson back to work, to the great benefit of the church.

In the meantime, having this collection of the metric rendering of the Psalms set to singable music is a rich resource for worship. This collection will be well received and happily utilized in many worship venues. The singing of this version of the Psalms will readily be praise to God; it will be at the same time a recurring thanks to Fred Anderson.

Walter Brueggemann
Columbia Theological Seminary

Preface

The genesis of this work goes back to my seminary days, to a class with Professor Bernhard Anderson at Princeton Theological Seminary. Dr. Anderson (no relation) reminded us that there would come a time in pastoral ministry when we found ourselves "dry" — not sure what to say or what to do about it. His prescribed remedy was the psalms — begin praying them. In the fall of 1982, nine years into ministry, and four years into my second pastorate, I found myself on the verge of what we now call "burnout" — too many meetings, stewardship and capital campaigns, conferences, denominational work, speaking engagements and the like, with no time in scripture beyond sermon preparation, and no time to nourish my soul. It was then I remembered what Dr. Anderson had said, and I turned to the psalms.

Trained as a singer and choral conductor, I knew the psalms best from singing them. Knowing the role metrical psalms had played in the life of John Calvin, at a similar time of crisis in his pastoral life in Strasbourg, I decided to try my hand at metering psalms in paraphrase as a daily prayer discipline. Soon, I found myself able to meter a psalm in a week (I still stand in awe of Isaac Watts, who reportedly metered one each morning before breakfast!). First thing, Monday mornings, and each day thereafter, as I closed my study door, there on the desk was a yellow pad (pre-computer days!) and as many English versions as I could find (which then were few) spread out before me. I would read each version aloud, listening to the rhythm of the texts, searching rhyme, appreciating the Hebrew parallelisms, and identifying the natural thematic breaks for versification. Then I began to fill the page with possible phrases that expressed the verses' meaning. Sometimes it was simply a direct quote. At other times it was a paraphrase, but always, it was an attempt to make the words sing, and singable. One of the particular gifts of years of singing is that I knew, almost by instinct, what would "fit in the mouth" and what would not, and that words with more than four syllables almost always had to be rejected. At the same time, I searched for a tune that seemed to match the psalm's sentiment, but one that was also well known by the congregation, for I wanted the psalms to be sung in worship.

The search for authentic meaning and rhyme took me to the Hebrew text and dictionary to find what lay behind certain key words. Though my Hebrew was anything but good enough to work with the basic text, I found that commentaries, dictionaries, interlinears, and much later, computer programs were all of enormous help, not only in clarifying meaning, but also in stimulating my mind in search of just the right word. By midweek, a coherent text was emerging, and I began to sing it as I wrote, to ensure that not only the rhyme but also the accents were correct. By the end of the week,

I had a draft complete. At the urging of my colleague, Donald L. Clapper (now of blessed memory), the Minister of Music at Pine Street, we printed the texts in the Sunday order of worship, between the Old Testament and Epistle Lessons, cited with a well-known tune, and began introducing metrical psalm singing to our congregation. As we sang, I had my pencil in hand, ready to make corrections and changes, which were then taken back to the study after worship and incorporated in a final text. Over the course of that first year, some twenty-plus new metrical psalms emerged, but more important still, the "dryness" was gone. In my work, I had found myself ever more deeply immersed in the prayers of the people of God, bathed in centuries of praise, lament, confession, wisdom, and proclamation. But more, my soul was being nourished and renewed, just as the psalms themselves promise when we address ourselves to God in conscious prayer.

When I began this task, I was committed to using inclusive language, seeing to it that no masculine references were used for the human family. Initially, I used masculine pronouns for God, but when the Psalter Task Force of the Presbyterian Church (USA) became aware of my work, and asked me to meter several texts for them, I attempted to take on their goal of no masculine pronouns for God, not only to meet their standards, but in an attempt to see if poetry might be written within that guideline while maintaining theological integrity as well as aesthetic appeal — one can use "God" again and again in a sentence as a substitute for "him" but it soon becomes deadly wooden! But what about "King" and "Lord"? To my own mind, the nouns "King" and "Lord" are so thoroughly biblical that they were not to be avoided. Further, the word "Lord" in contemporary North American usage almost always refers to God. For that reason I have continued to use "Lord" and "God" interchangeably.

By 1985, some fifty texts had been metered, and through the gracious support of people like Arlo Duba, Herold Daniels (now of blessed memory), Hal H. Hopson, James G. Kirk, and Clements E. Lamberth Jr. (also of blessed memory) the texts were beginning to be sung at General Assemblies, worship conferences, and in other Presbyterian congregations interested in liturgical renewal. It was through their encouragement that the work came to the attention of Keith Crim, who was then Editorial Director at Westminster Press. I am indebted to Keith for his encouragement, advice, assistance, and support, as well as his skill as an editor, Hebrew scholar, and translator. In 1986, under his direction, my collection of fifty metrical psalms was published under the title *Singing Psalms of Joy and Praise*. That psalter came into the hands of the committee working on a new hymnal, as it was committed to returning metrical psalm singing to our tradition, and they included fifteen of those texts in *The Presbyterian Hymnal, 1990*.

Two years later I was called to be pastor of Madison Avenue Presbyterian Church in New York City, and in collaboration with organist and Director of Music John Weaver, and after John, Dr. Andrew E. Henderson, my work on the psalms continued. By then, I had written some eighty or ninety texts, but, because they had been crafted over a period of seventeen years, they were scattered widely across the three-year lectionary cycle — there were lots of gaps! It was then I determined to use part of my summer study/sermon planning leave to intentionally work on new texts, initially, for those that were missing, either from the new hymnal, or my own collection, but later for the whole three-year cycle itself. For the next ten years I would use my morning prayer time at our summer home in New Hampshire to meter psalms for congregational use the next year. I did so until I had completed all of the psalms and canticles appointed in the three-year cycle. By the summer of 2012 I had finished the project. It was then that I learned what every author and writer ultimately learns: it is easier to create material than it is to find someone to publish it!

With the psalter project complete, and as I continued to look for a publisher, I took on a new morning-prayer discipline, blogging through the lessons in the two-year daily lectionary. Soon, I was posting these on the church's website for the congregation's devotional use. Each day I would write a reflection on the four lessons for the day: Old Testament, Psalm, Epistle, and Gospel. Over the several years, I completed that two-year cycle twice. The result was a pastoral reflection on each of the texts, which meant, among other things, a pastoral commentary-reflection on each of the psalms.

For several years Bill Eerdmans had been pressing me to write something for him, and we had considered several possible book ideas, but the psalm project and then the daily blog always got in the way. It was over lunch in the fall of 2013, with Bill and mutual friend Norman Hjelm, that we talked about the possibility of printing the text of the metered psalms along with the pastoral reflections, and this work began. I owe an enormous debt to Bill and Norman, along with the others I have mentioned here, especially, in the last ten years, to Dr. Andrew E. Henderson, my colleague at Madison Avenue, who judiciously has used his skills to set the texts to hymns' melodic lines for printing in the Sunday order of worship. Also, a special word of thanks to Jennifer Hoffman, Senior Project Editor at Eerdmans, for her careful eye and "well tuned ear" that was always most helpful. Finally, I am extraordinarily thankful to Walter Brueggemann, for his helpful and gracious foreword, and most of all, to the saints at both Pine Street and Madison Avenue Presbyterian Church for their constant support and encouragement.

What I have learned in metering the psalm texts and reflecting upon them pastorally is that within the psalter there is the whole of the gospel of God. I have often thought of the psalter as the first testament's gospel, as so much of the gospel of God sings forth from it. Professor Brueggemann is right in his concern that so many of the laments have been avoided in popular psalmody and especially in the three-year lectionary. One of the most challenging texts for me to meter was Psalm 130, but there are more. My task now is to complete the psalter, with metrical versions for all 150 of them.

In the reflections following each metered psalm or canticle, the reader may note that I rely on standard Bible translations, particularly the New Revised Standard Version.

John Calvin wrote that praying the psalms was talking to God using God's own words. In this day when so many have tried to push God to the

xii

margins, or have tried to domesticate God to "my God," the psalms stand before us as both invitation and challenge: to praise the Lord, to be still and know God, to wait on the Lord, and to welcome God into the most intimate and painful portions of our lives, knowing that as we do, God will come and fill us with the Spirit, and draw us ever more deeply into the mystery of the good news of God's love, mercy, grace, renewing, and sustaining presence.

FRED R. ANDERSON
Madison Avenue Presbyterian Church
Ash Wednesday, 2015

Singing the Psalms in Metered, Versified Text

It was the sixteenth-century Protestant reformer Martin Luther who initiated the practice of writing hymn texts to be sung to well-known secular tunes. The tradition of singing psalms, following Luther's lead, emerged shortly thereafter in Strasbourg. French court poet Claude Marot, living among French exiles in Strasbourg, paraphrased psalm texts into French, setting them in poetic form so they could then be sung to well-known tunes. It was there, between 1538 and 1541, that John Calvin, while in exile from Geneva, first heard metrical psalm-singing by a congregation.

Calvin was powerfully moved upon hearing his Strasbourg congregation singing the psalms in their own language, and he enthusiastically endorsed and supported the practice as a central part of a congregation's participation in worship. The original Strasbourg psalter contained twelve psalms by Marot, to which Calvin added several more texts of his own composition, as well as the Ten Commandments, the Song of Simeon, and the Apostles' Creed. All of this was for the congregation's use, and the psalter appeared under the title *Aulcuns Pseaumes et cantiques mys en chant*.

In 1541 Calvin returned to Geneva, taking the Strasbourg Psalter with him. By the end of 1542, Marot had become a refugee in Geneva, and while there he contributed nineteen more psalm texts. Louis Bourgeois, also a refugee, lived and taught music in Geneva for sixteen years, and Calvin took the opportunity to use Bourgeois's hymn tunes with additional psalm versifications, the most famous being the OLD HUNDREDTH. Thus, the texts of Marot and Calvin and the tunes collected and arranged by Bourgeois created the Geneva Psalter, which by 1562 included versification of all 150 psalm texts.

The practice of congregational singing of metered psalms, so central to sixteenth-century Reformed worship, made its way from Geneva across the lands embracing the Genevan reform movement into Scotland, the Netherlands, England, and, finally, America with the coming of Scots Presbyterians and English Puritans. In fact, the first book published in America was a metrical psalter — The Bay Psalter — produced in 1640. Metrical psalmody has been called the Reformed tradition's greatest contribution to Christian worship.

What is a metrical psalm? The simplest answer is this: a poetic paraphrase of a biblical psalm text, set in contemporary, vernacular language, versified in strict meter, and usually rhymed, so that it can be sung to a well-known tune of the same metrical setting.

Metrical settings are characterized and named by the number of syllables in each line and the number of lines in each stanza (there is no limit to stanzas, but three to five are quite normal).

A Short Meter text/tune (SM) has four lines, the first, second, and fourth lines made up of six syllables, with the third line built on eight. Thus the metrical designation for Short Meter (SM) is 6.6.8.6. The well-known hymn "Blest Be the Tie That Binds" is a Short Meter text:

> Blest be the tie that binds (6 syllables)
> Our hearts in Christian love. (6 syllables)
> The fellowship of kindred hearts (8 syllables)
> Is like to that above. (6 syllables)

Notice that the second and fourth lines rhyme.

The most common metrical pattern is 8.6.8.6, suitably called Common Meter (CM). It has eight syllables in the first line, six in the second, eight in the third, and six in the fourth, generally with the second and fourth lines rhyming. Isaac Watts, the great eighteenth-century hymn text author, used Common Meter for his well-known hymn "O God, Our Help in Ages Past," set to the Common Meter tune named ST. ANNE.

> O God, our help in ages past, (8 syllables)
> Our hope for years to come. (6 syllables)
> Our shelter from the stormy blast, (8 syllables)
> And our eternal home. (6 syllables)

This pattern can be doubled from four to eight lines, and when that is done it is known as Common Meter Doubled (CMD): 8.6.8.6.8.6.8.6. "It Came upon a Midnight Clear" is a Common Meter Doubled text set to the appropriately named tune CAROL.

Long Meter (LM) consists of four lines of eight syllables each, and it is designated 8.8.8.8. It is the structure used by the sixteenth-century English psalm text author William Kethe in his paraphrase of Psalm 100, "All People That on Earth Do Dwell," set to the Long Meter Geneva tune suitably titled OLD HUNDREDTH. The tune is attributed to Louis Bourgeois, Calvin's musician for the Geneva Psalter.

And, of course, Long Meter can be doubled (LMD).

There are other metrical patterns as well: 7.6.7.6, 7.6.7.6 D, 7.7.7.7, even 10.10.10.10.10 and 11.11.11.11, and irregular patterns like 8.7.8.7.7.7 or 6.4.6.4.10.10. A look at the Metrical Index of Tunes in the back of any hymnal will reveal the wide diversity of possible settings, each with its own rhyming pattern and particular form of accent. Each is categorized by the number of syllables per line and the number of lines in a stanza. Sometimes, the numerical designation is followed by "with refrain" or "with alleluias," all of which also have a metrical pattern to them.

One other word: although, generally, a text of a certain metrical pattern can be sung to another tune of the same meter, be sure to check that the accents match. Not all tunes within a given metrical setting have the same accents, and you may find yourself "singING" instead of "SINGing."

The Psalms and Canticles Appointed in the Common Lectionary (Revised)

See *Book of Common Worship* (Louisville: Westminster John Knox Press, 1993), 1037–48.

	Year A	Year B	Year C
Advent 1	Psalm 122	Psalm 80:1–7, 17–19	Psalm 25:1–10
Advent 2	Psalm 72:1–7, 18–19	Psalm 85:1–2, 8–13	Luke 1:68–79
Advent 3	Psalm 146:5–10	Psalm 126	Isaiah 12:2–6
Advent 4	Psalm 80:1–7, 17–19	Psalm 89:1–4, 19–26	Luke 1:47–55 or Psalm 80:1–7
Christmas Eve	Psalm 96	Psalm 96	Psalm 96
Christmas Day	Psalm 97	Psalm 97	Psalm 97
Nativity of Jesus	Psalm 98	Psalm 98	Psalm 98
Christmas 1	Psalm 148	Psalm 148	Psalm 148
Christmas 2	Psalm 147:12–20	Psalm 147:12–20	Psalm 147:12–20
Epiphany	Psalm 72:1–7, 10–14	Psalm 72:1–7, 10–14	Psalm 72:1–7, 10–14
Baptism	Psalm 29	Psalm 29	Psalm 29
2nd Sunday OT (ordinary time)	Psalm 40:1–11	Psalm 139:1–6, 13–18	Psalm 36:5–10
3rd Sunday OT	Psalm 27:1, 4–9	Psalm 62:5–12	Psalm 19
4th Sunday OT	Psalm 15	Psalm 111	Psalm 71:1–6
5th Sunday OT	Psalm 112:1–10	Psalm 147:1–11, 20c	Psalm 138
6th Sunday OT	Psalm 119:1–8	Psalm 30	Psalm 1

	Year A	Year B	Year C
7th Sunday OT	Psalm 119:33–40	Psalm 41	Psalm 37:1–11, 39–40
8th Sunday OT	Psalm 131	Psalm 103:1–13, 22	Psalm 92:1–4, 12–15
Transfiguration	Psalm 2 or 99	Psalm 50:1–6	Psalm 99
Ash Wednesday	Psalm 51:1–17 or Isaiah 58:1–12	Psalm 51	Psalm 51
Lent 1	Psalm 32	Psalm 25:1–10	Psalm 91:1–2, 9–16
Lent 2	Psalm 121	Psalm 103:1–13, 22	Psalm 27:1–9, 10–14
Lent 3	Psalm 95	Psalm 19	Psalm 63:1–8
Lent 4	Psalm 23	Psalm 107:1–3, 17–22	Psalm 32
Lent 5	Psalm 130	Psalm 51:1–12	Psalm 126
Palm Sunday	Psalm 118:1–2, 19–29	Psalm 118:1–2, 19–29	Psalm 118:1–2, 19–29
Passion Sunday	Psalm 31:9–16	Psalm 31:9–16	Psalm 31:9–16
Monday, Holy Week	Psalm 36:5–11	Psalm 36:5–11	Psalm 36:5–11
Tuesday, Holy Week	Psalm 71:1–14	Psalm 71:1–14	Psalm 71:1–14
Wednesday, Holy Week	Psalm 70	Psalm 70	Psalm 70
Maundy Thursday	Psalm 116:1–2, 12–19	Psalm 116:1–2, 12–19	Psalm 116:1–2, 12–19
Good Friday	Psalm 22	Psalm 22	Psalm 22
Easter	Psalm 118:1–2, 14–24	Psalm 118:1–2, 14–24	Psalm 118:1–2, 14–24
Easter Evening	Psalm 114	Psalm 114	Psalm 114
Easter 2	Psalm 16	Psalm 93	Psalm 118:14–29
Easter 3	Psalm 116:1–4, 12–19	Psalm 4, two versions	Psalm 30
Easter 4	Psalm 23	Psalm 23	Psalm 23
Easter 5	Psalm 31:1–3, 15–16	Psalm 22:25–31	Psalm 148
Easter 6	Psalm 66:8–20	Psalm 98	Psalm 67
Ascension	Psalm 47	Psalm 92	Psalm 93

	Year A	Year B	Year C
Easter 7	Psalm 68:1–10, 32–35	Psalm 1	Psalm 97
Pentecost	Psalm 104:24–34, 35b	Psalm 104:24–34, 35b	Psalm 104:24–34, 35b
Trinity	Psalm 8	Psalm 29	Psalm 8
9th Sunday OT	Psalm 46	Psalm 139:1–6, 13–18	Psalm 96
10th Sunday OT	Psalm 33:1–12	Psalm 138	Psalm 146
11th Sunday OT	Psalm 116:1–2, 12–19	Psalm 20	Psalm 5:1–8
12th Sunday OT	Psalm 86:1–10, 16–17	Psalm 9:9–20	Psalms 42 and 43
13th Sunday OT	Psalm 13	Psalm 130	Psalm 77:1–2, 11–20
14th Sunday OT	Psalm 45:10–17	Psalm 48	Psalm 30
15th Sunday OT	Psalm 119:105–12	Psalm 24	Psalm 82
16th Sunday OT	Psalm 139:1–12, 23–24	Psalm 89:20–37	Psalm 52
17th Sunday OT	Psalm 105:1–11, 45b, or Ps. 128	Psalm 14	Psalm 85
18th Sunday OT	Psalm 17:1–7, 15	Psalm 51:1–12	Psalm 107:1–9, 43
19th Sunday OT	Psalm 105:1–6, 16–22	Psalm 130	Psalm 50:1–8, 22–23
20th Sunday OT	Psalm 133	Psalm 111	Psalm 80:1–2, 8–19
21st Sunday OT	Psalm 124	Psalm 84	Psalm 71:1–6
22nd Sunday OT	Psalm 105:1–6, 23–26	Psalm 45:1–2, 6–9	Psalm 81:1, 10–16
23rd Sunday OT	Psalm 149	Psalm 125	Psalm 139:1–6, 13–18
24th Sunday OT	Psalm 114	Psalm 19	Psalm 14
25th Sunday OT	Psalm 105:1–6, 37–45	Psalm 1	Psalm 79:1–9
26th Sunday OT	Psalm 78:1–4, 12–16	Psalm 124	Psalm 91:1–6, 14–16

	Year A	Year B	Year C
27th Sunday OT	Psalm 19	Psalm 26	Lamentations 3:19–26, or Psalm 137
28th Sunday OT	Psalm 106:1–6, 19–23	Psalm 22:1–15	Psalm 66:1–12
29th Sunday OT	Psalm 99	Psalm 104:1–9, 24, 35c	Psalm 119:97–104
30th Sunday OT	Psalm 90:1–6, 13–17	Psalm 34:1–8 (19–22)	Psalm 65
31st Sunday OT	Psalm 107:1–7, 33–37	Psalm 146	Psalm 119:137–44
All Saints	Psalm 34:1–10, 22	Psalm 24	Psalm 149
32nd Sunday OT	Psalm 78:1–7	Psalm 127	Psalm 145:1–5, 17–21
33rd Sunday OT	Psalm 123	1 Samuel 2:1–10	Isaiah 12
Christ the King	Psalm 100	Psalm 132:1–12 (13–18)	Luke 1:68–79

PSALMS

Psalm 1

CM
DUNFERMLINE

The blest are those whose footsteps shun
    The path the sinful walk,
Whose lives turn from all wickedness,
    Whose mouths avoid loose talk.

In God's instructions they find health,
    His laws are their delight.
They meditate upon this word
    In thanks both day and night.

Like mighty trees by flowing streams
    Their living bears good fruit.
There is no dryness in their lives,
    No weakness at their root.

The wicked sing a different song,
    Like dried-up leaves they blow
From place to place with no true joy;
    In emptiness they go.

Before the Lord they will not stand,
    That judgment is secure;
Nor in the company of saints
    Can their works long endure.

You, Lord our God, still bless our days;
    With fullness they do teem.
All those who ground their lives in you
    Shall find the living stream.

Psalm 1 begins the entire collection of psalms with a celebration of God's gift of Torah, and a reflection on two ways of life: one centered and nurtured by the "law of the Lord," the other surrounded by scoffers and sinners; one righteous, the other wicked. The former are like trees planted near streams of water, deeply rooted, richly nurtured, and produce fruit in their season. The latter are like chaff during threshing; the wind simply drives it away because it has no substance. The wicked will not withstand the judgment or be among the congregation of the righteous because the Lord watches over the righteous, while the wicked perish.

Psalm 2

7.7.7.7 D

ABERYSTWYTH, HINTZE

Why are nations grumbling,
    And conspiring plots in vain?
Rulers of the world rise up,
    Weaving webs of death and pain.
Then against the Lord they cry,
    And against God's Holy Son,
"Let us tear their bonds from us,
    And with their control be done."

But the Lord has scorn on them,
    Laughing and enthroned on high;
God brings wrath upon their work,
    Filled with anger God replies:
"It is my own holy will
    That the Christ on earth shall reign,
And on Zion's holy hill
    My anointed I'll maintain."

God's decree unto the King
    Tells us what the Lord did say:
"You are my own holy child,
    I've begotten you this day.
Ask of me and I will make
    All the nations your own stay.
These possessions you shall rule,
    Strong as iron smashing clay."

Therefore leaders of the earth,
    Serve the Lord with holy fear;
Trembling come before the throne,
    Or God's anger will appear.

Kiss God's feet in trembling awe,
　　Or the Lord will use the rod,
Making beggars of all kings.
　　Blest are those who trust in God.

Psalm 2 is the first in a series of royal psalms, probably used at the annual reenactment of the king's enthronement, reminding him that he is God's viceroy, God's anointed, and God's own adopted son. The nations can rage and conspire against him, but the Lord, for whom he reigns, sits in heaven laughing at them. God will speak to the king's enemies in wrath, reminding them that the king who reigns in Zion (Jerusalem) is there at God's hand and doing. Then the king repeats what the Lord has said to him, "You are my son; today I have begotten you. Ask of me, and I will make the nations your heritage, and the ends of the earth your possession. You shall break them with a rod of iron, and dash them in pieces like a potter's vessel." From this psalm the idea arose that Israel's king was the Lord's adopted son. The psalm then turns to the other rulers of the earth, warning them to hear and be wise. They too are called upon to serve the Lord with fear. All rulers of the earth are called on to reign under God's sovereign rule or experience God's judgment themselves. Happy are all who take refuge in him. After the loss of the monarchy in Israel, following the Babylonian captivity, the idea of the king as God's anointed (*meshiach*) began to develop into the notion of an ultimate Messiah-King who would appear and return God's reign to God's people. He would be known as "God's son" because he would inherit David's throne. The New Testament capitalized on this psalm as a means of identifying Jesus as that Messiah, but a Son of a different order than all the other kings of Israel — an ontological one — therefore the capital *S* in Son.

6

Psalm 4

8.7.8.7 D
RUSTINGTON

Lord, our help and our defender,
    God who comes to those who fall;
When in trouble or in danger,
    You are there to help us all.
Yet, with kindness and with caring,
    You respond to great and small.
Now, in your abundant mercy,
    Hear us as on you we call.

Those of substance and of comfort,
    Rich in things but poor in soul,
Now in silent contemplation,
    Hear these words to make you whole:
Know the Lord supports the loyal,
    From such love do not depart.
Those who chase life's vain illusions
    Fall to falsehood's subtle art.

Many look to you for blessings.
    "Give us what we want!" they pray.
"Look on us with loving kindness,
    Give success in every way."
But you give us joy far greater
    Than mere wealth can ever pay.
Lord, you give us peace and safety,
    Guarding life both night and day.

P salm 4 is an individual plea for God's help that incorporates elements
of lament as well as expressions of confidence in God's care. It alternates between talking to God and talking to others and falls into instruc-

tion in wisdom along the way. God has responded to the psalmist's former distress; the plea is for God's graciousness now. The psalmist now turns to those around him asking, how long should they be allowed to cause his honor to suffer shame? How long will they love vain words and seek after lies? Let them know that the Lord has set apart the faithful for himself, and clearly, the psalmist considers himself among the faithful. He says, "The Lord hears when I call to him." Now the psalmist offers instruction; is it to himself or to those around him? "When you are disturbed, do not sin; ponder on your beds, and be silent. Offer right sacrifices and put your trust in the Lord." Once again the psalmist turns to the Lord, telling him that there are many who search after signs of God's goodness and plead for God's face to shine upon them (with reference to the Aaronic benediction, Num. 6:24–25). Affirming that God has put gladness in his own heart, more than when grain and wine abound, he can now lie down this night in safety and sleep in peace. Only the Lord gives such care. This final phrase suggests that the psalm was intended for use in night prayer, as it is regularly used in the Christian tradition today. A lovely paraphrase of this last verse is used in a night prayer liturgy: "In the night I can take my rest; you alone keep my life secure."

Psalm 5

LM

WAREHAM

As morning dawns, Lord, hear our cry.
    O Sovereign God, now hear our sigh.
As first light brings the sun's warm rays,
    Accept our sacrifice of praise.

Before you, Lord, the wicked fall,
    And none shall dwell within your hall.
The proud shall never gain a place,
    Nor evil live to see your face.

Your steadfast love shall welcome all
    Who seek your house and on you call.
O lead us, Lord, in righteousness,
    As through this day your name we bless.

Let all who seek you then rejoice,
    And sing to you with joyful voice.
For you shall bless the righteous, Lord.
    Forever be your name adored.

Psalm 5, traditionally used in Morning Prayer, pleads for God's protection and care against the psalmist's enemies. Knowing that God abhors wickedness and the boastful, the psalmist expresses the certainty that because of God's steadfast love, he will again be able to enter God's house to worship, even as he bows down toward the temple in awe. His enemies are full of lies, and their deceit and rebellion are really rebellion against God. Let them bear the fruit of their guilt, and fall by their own counsel. On the other hand, let all who take refuge in the Lord rejoice. Let them sing forever. Pleading for the Lord to spread his protection over all who take refuge in him, the psalmist ends as he begins, expressing joyful confidence in the Lord's blessings and care for those who are righteous (in a right relationship with God and one another). Cover them with divine favor as a shield.

9

Psalm 8

CM

WINCHESTER OLD

O Lord, our God, how excellent,
    How glorious is your name.
Your majesty surrounds the earth
    And children sing your fame.

The heavens shout your handiwork,
    We stand beneath in awe,
To think the one who made all things,
    Should care for us at all.

Yet you have made us less than gods,
    Surpassing all but you.
With heart and mind, with strength and will,
    To search for what is true.

Into our hands you've placed all things.
    The earth, the sea; each place,
We're called to probe for secret gifts
    And venture into space.

O Lord, our God, how excellent,
    How glorious is your name,
Majestic in your holiness,
    We sing and praise your fame.

Psalm 8 reflects on the majesty of the Lord who is sovereign over all things, and the majesty of humankind whom God has made just a little less than himself — and that is worthy of serious thought! It begins with praise directed to God whose name is regal and magnificent in all the earth. God's glory is above the heavens and far superior to it. God is so wondrous that something as natural as the babbling of babies forms a bulwark and silences God's foes. Then the psalmist, taking in the glory of creation, especially the celestial majesty, wonders aloud what it means that the one who made all of this also made us, and just a little less than himself, at that. But more, God is not only mindful of us, but cares for us. This is the language that lies behind the notion of our being created in the image of God in Genesis with dominion over the rest of creation (Gen. 1:26–30), as this psalm is much older than that first creation account. The psalm ends with the same refrain of praise with which it began, "O Lord, our Lord" (the Hebrew is *Adonai,* not *melech*), a far more personal term of affection for God. This is a psalm to be prayed on a brilliant, starlit night or at a glorious sunset. It also reminds us of our place and role in God's creation. What is it about us that truly is unique?

Psalm 9

Verses 9–20
8.8.8.8.8.8
MELITA, ST. CATHERINE, OLD 113TH

O Refuge for the world's oppressed,
    Your name is known by all distressed.
All those who trust you in their fear
    Are not forsaken; you are near.
Come join in song to praise the Lord,
    Who dwells in Zion, most adored.

Your mercy sees the misery
    My enemies have brought on me.
O lift me from the gates of death,
    So praise might fill my every breath.
And standing in your holy gate,
    Sing of salvation true and great.

The nations sink in their own schemes,
    Enmeshed in their own evil dreams.
The wicked live within the net,
    Ensnared in evil traps they set.
For you have made your presence known
    And brought forth justice for your own.

The wicked who forget your name
    Shall die surrounded by their shame.
While needs are met among the poor
    And hope remains an open door.
Rise up, O Lord, and judge the earth;
    Remind us of our mortal birth.

Psalm 9 is a psalm that gives thanks to the Lord for continuing protection and salvation. Though it might appear a royal psalm, the enemies being other nations, we never hear the voice in the prayer identified as the king's, as it would be in a royal psalm. Rather it simply focuses on God's ability to respond, whether "present" or afar, to scatter the wicked and maintain the just person's cause. Verses 1 through 8 offer thanksgiving for God's wonderful deeds, for deliverance from particular enemies, praise for the rebuke of other nations and the wicked and affirmation that the Lord is enthroned forever and his throne is a throne of judgment. Verse 9 affirms that the Lord is a stronghold for the oppressed who seek him. These he will not forsake. After calling for praise in Zion, the psalmist turns to personal intercession and deliverance from those who hate him. Again, there is recollection of God's judgment on the nations that have been caught in their own net. The wicked are consigned to Sheol while the needy shall "not always be forgotten, nor the hope of the poor taken away," one of the high and memorable phrases from this psalm. Finally, God is called upon to "Rise up," judge the nations, and put them in their place — they are only human. *Se'lah* is a word that appears to call upon a musical chorus of praise from the temple musicians, whether instrumental or vocal. Because this is an acrostic psalm, beginning each successive section with the next letter of the Hebrew alphabet, the flow of ideas can seem a bit jumbled. It can seem that two psalms have been joined into one: the first, a psalm of thanksgiving; the second, a petition for help. And because Psalm 10 has no introductory material, some believe Psalm 9 and Psalm 10 were originally one. In fact, they appear as one in both the Septuagint (Greek translation of the Old Testament) and the Roman Catholic Vulgate Bible, which used the Septuagint to make the Latin translation.

Psalm 10

Verses 12–18

CM

RICHMOND, DUTTON (© Hal H. Hopson)

Arise, O Lord, lift up your hand;
 Our pain and hurt redress.
Your faithful look to you for help;
 Come heal our present stress.

Why do the wicked mock your name,
 And claim you have no pow'r?
They tell themselves you take no count
 Of evil in this hour.

But you observe, and you do see
 Our trouble and our grief.
Within your hands you take it, Lord;
 You give your saints relief.

The helpless look to you for strength
 To shatter evil's wrong.
O break the grip of wicked ones,
 Till all their work is gone.

You, Lord, are sovereign over all,
 Just rule is your command.
All godless people here on earth
 Will perish from the land.

O Lord, you hear our cry for help;
 On you we can rely.
You give us strength so none on earth
 Shall harm or terrify.

Psalm 10 pleads for God to intervene against the evils of the wicked who oppress the poor. The evils are set forth in vivid detail in the first half of this psalm, which then calls upon God to respond as the poor's only source of defense against them. But first, the eternal question: Why is God remote in all of this; why does God hide in times of trouble? In arrogance the wicked persecute the poor, boasting in the desires of their greedy hearts, and curse and renounce the Lord, saying "There is no God," the proverbial creed of fools. Yet, the other proverbial questions: Why do they prosper, why are they allowed to ambush and murder the innocent and, like a lion, seize the poor and the helpless and drag them off to their dens? In their hearts they think that God has either forgotten, or has simply looked the other way. After a long rehearsal of their wickedness, the psalmist cries out, "Rise up, O Lord; O God, lift up your hand; do not forget the oppressed!" The Lord does see, does note trouble and grief in order to take it into his hands. "The helpless commit themselves to you, you who have been the helper of orphans. Break the arm of the wicked; seek out their wickedness until you find none." This is followed by a confession of faith: "The Lord is king forever and ever." Nations perish from his land. And now, with a word of hopeful confidence the psalm proclaims that the Lord will hear the desire of the meek and strengthen their hearts. The Lord will hear and do justice for the orphan and the oppressed, so that those from the earth who strike terror may do so no more.

Psalm 14

LM

PENTECOST

"There is no God," the foolish say,
    And so they live in their own way.
Corrupt and shameful things they do,
    Without regard, O Lord, for you.

You look upon us constantly,
    For wisdom — true humanity.
But there is none, few stop to pray;
    Pursuing wealth, all go astray.

But terror stands in evil's way,
    For you are with all who obey.
Those who confound the faithful's plan
    Confront your strong, protecting hand.

And so we pray for victory.
    Come, Lord! From Zion, make us free.
How happy shall your people be
    When you restore prosperity.

Psalm 14 is a condemnation of those who say, "There is no God," who as a result are both corrupt and lack any moral compass whatsoever. Though seeing themselves wise in their own eyes, they are fools. There are few stronger words of personal condemnation in the Old Testament than "fool!" In wisdom literature it is the term for the "empty headed," but it is less about thoughtless, imprudent behavior than about the orientation of one's life. Though in this psalm, the "fool" is defined as one who says there is no God, this is less a question about whether or not there is a god, than the question of whether a god even cares. After all, they are corrupt and do abominable deeds; there is no one who does good. It is one of the earliest affirmations of what will come to be known in Reformed theology as "total depravity." But the Lord looks down from heaven on humankind to see if there are any who are wise. The verdict is "No!" All have gone astray; all are perverse; no one does good. They have no knowledge (here, more about relationship with God than information about God), fail to call upon him, and eat up God's people as though they were bread. The psalm now describes their fate: they shall be in great terror, for God is with the company of the righteous. Those who would confuse and abuse the poor should know that the Lord is the refuge of the poor; in abusing them, they abuse God. The psalm ends with a plea that deliverance for Israel will come from the Lord; it acknowledges that when that does occur, and the Lord restores the fortunes of his people, Jacob will rejoice. Notice that nowhere in this psalm is the Lord addressed. Rather, this seems to be a psalm intended to drive home the conviction that God is looking, God does care, and God will act against those who, in their wickedness, abuse the poor and fail to recognize or serve the Lord. The conviction is repeated, virtually verbatim, in Psalm 53.

Psalm 15

8.6.8.6.8.6

MORNING SONG, CORONATION, CAROL'S GIFT

Lord, who may dwell within your tent,
 Upon your holy hill?
All those whose walk is without blame,
 Whose lives are upright still;
Who speak the truth from their own hearts,
 And seek to do your will.

No slander comes forth from their tongue,
 No evil from their deeds.
They are not wicked to their friends,
 But hearken to their pleas.
Their neighbors need not fear their scorn,
 But trust them for their needs.

The wicked have no place with them;
 Their deeds they do despise.
While those who truly fear the Lord
 Are honored as the wise.
They keep their oath at their own hurt;
 They cannot live with lies.

They lend their money without cost;
 No interest do they seek.
A bribe is loathsome to their minds;
 How could they wrong the meek?
And thus they stand immovable,
 As your sure way they keep.

18

P salm 15 was written as a liturgy of entrance to the temple, but may also have been used to teach the way of life expected of those who want to live within God's presence. Once the question is asked as to who may dwell in God's tent, eleven answers are given: walk blamelessly, do what is right, speak the truth, do not slander, do no evil to friends, do not shame a friend, despise the wicked, honor those who fear the Lord, stand by your oaths, even at the cost of your own hurt or loss, do not charge interest, and do not take a bribe against the innocent. Those who do these things shall never be moved. Then, as now in the Islamic community, charging interest on a loan was strictly forbidden because it took advantage of another's need.

Psalm 16

CM

ST. FLAVIN, ARLINGTON

Preserve us, Lord, for you are God,
    And Refuge is your name.
Apart from you there is no good,
    And life is turned to shame.

But all the false gods of this world,
    Who tempt us for our praise,
Bring sorrow, pain, and your contempt,
    To all who walk their ways.

You give us daily all we need,
    And look to our distress;
Our cup is filled with pleasant things,
    As our own lives you bless.

We bless you for your heart's own thought,
    For counsel that is true;
With you the center of our days,
    Our lives shall not be moved.

Our hearts are glad, our lives rejoice,
    In you we dwell secure.
For nothing can destroy our lives;
    Your Spirit holds us sure.

You lead us in the path of life,
    And bring us joy unknown;
Eternal life you've promised all
    Who claim you for their own.

P salm 16 is a psalm of trust that acknowledges the Lord as not only a refuge, but the source of all good in life. The psalmist looks to the holy ones — the saints — for guidance and fellowship while not willing even to speak the names of those who serve and worship other gods. With the Lord at the center of life — the chosen portion — the dimensions of life have fallen in "pleasant places," delivering a goodly heritage. Therefore the psalm blesses the Lord who gives constant counsel. Keeping the Lord always at the center means not being overcome or defeated. Rather, heart, soul and body rejoice, are glad and rest secure, for God does not give up his faithful ones to Sheol or the Pit. Rather, God reveals the path of life. In God's presence there is fullness of joy, and pleasures for evermore.

Psalm 17

Verses 1–7, 15
7.6.7.6 D
LLANGLOFFAN

O Lord, now hear my pleading;
    To you I come in trust.
Now judge in my own favor,
    For Lord, my cause is just.
You know my heart, my purpose;
    Within there is no wrath.
I speak no word of evil;
    I walk no violent path.

I always choose your pathway;
    From it I will not stray.
I come to you for justice;
    Respond, Lord, be my stay.
Reveal your love, O Savior,
    To all who seek your grace,
And satisfied, I'll 'waken,
    Beholding your own face.

P salm 17 is a plea for deliverance that begins with the lament of the innocent, calling on God for deliverance, and ends with assurance that God will do it. The psalmist declares his innocence, with lips free from deceit, and invites God's night visitation to try his heart and test him. God will find no wickedness in him. He has avoided the ways of the violent and held fast to God's paths. And so, he calls upon God to listen, to show steadfast love and guard him as "the apple of your eye," hiding him "in the shadow of your wings"; both are powerful poetic images of God's intimate care. The one who prays is surrounded by pitiless enemies who speak arrogantly and like a lion, track him down as their prey, eager to ambush and tear him apart. And so the call comes for God to "rise up, confront, and overthrow them!" "By your sword deliver my life from the wicked." His enemies' only concern is their bellies. He pleads, "Fill them with what you have in store for them" — God's vengeance!

Psalm 18

CMD

FOREST GREEN, RESIGNATION

I love you, Lord, my strength, my rock,
    My fortress and my aid.
My refuge and salvation's hope,
    To you I long have prayed.
Though cords and snares encompassed me,
    Confronting me with death,
In my distress I called to you,
    My life and source of breath.

In your own courts you heard my plea;
    My crying reached your ear.
The mountains shook, foundations reeled;
    Your anger strikes such fear.
You came to me on wings of wind,
    With storm and lightning's pow'r.
You saved me from my enemies;
    You give me strength each hour.

Your statutes, Lord, I daily keep;
    My actions seek your will.
In loyalty I walk your way;
    My heart is steadfast still.
You pay the righteous with right things,
    Yet bring the haughty low.
A perfect shield for all in need,
    Destruction to your foe.

For who is God except the Lord,
My rock, my strength, my stay?
Salvation's shield you give to me;
You widen vict'ry's way.
Blest be your name, O Living God,
The vict'ry you have won.
Your name I will proclaim to all,
O Saving, Sovereign One.

Psalm 18 is introduced as a psalm of David, uttered when the Lord had rescued him from the hand of Saul. Scholars classify this as a "royal psalm of thanks for victory." But without the elaborate introduction between "To the leader . . ." and "I love you, O Lord . . . ," Psalm 18:1–20 is a classic expression of thanksgiving and praise for God's intervention in one's life, regardless of the circumstances or whether or not one is king. Notice how general the psalmist's troubles are: "cords of death encompass, torrents of perdition assail, cords of Sheol entangle, the snares of death confront." They could apply to anyone. There is simply unabashed love expressed for the Lord because of God's deliverance and salvation. From the temple in Jerusalem, the Lord has heard the psalmist's cry. Verses 7–15 use the familiar storm image to speak of God's presence and sovereignty. Such language was common in the religious language of the Canaanites as well, and may well have been appropriated from a Baal liturgy to make the point that it is the Lord who is sovereign even over those deities. Remember, at this stage, Israel was not monotheistic, but convinced that their God was the God of gods. This portion of the psalm concludes with the psalmist expressing the conviction that all this has taken place because God has rewarded the psalmist's integrity. It then returns to the theme of the blessings of keeping the ways of the Lord. This is the third-longest psalm in the collection, fifty verses in all. Only in that final verse do we learn that the psalmist is the king, the Lord's anointed.

Psalm 19

CMD

KINGSFOLD, SHEPHERD'S PIPES

The heav'ns, O Lord, proclaim your pow'r;
  Creation sings your fame.
The handiwork of all the world
  Speaks of your holy name.
Each day breaks forth with its own song;
  Night follows with its mirth.
Their melodies are sweet and strong,
  Resounding through the earth.

The heav'ns are like a well-pitched tent,
  Spread firmly o'er the earth,
From which the sun breaks forth with strength,
  To bring the day to birth.
That living law which calls it forth
  Revives the weary soul.
Its witness to your glorious works
  Gives hope and makes us whole.

Your law is perfect and secure;
  It makes our hearts rejoice.
Like precious gold, like honeycomb,
  It is a priceless choice.
In keeping it we find reward,
  Of life, and strength, and health.
These come to those who keep your law;
  Can there be greater wealth?

We cannot, Lord, discern our faults,
    Nor know how much we err.
So keep us from unthinking sin,
    That your life we may share.
So let our words and all our thoughts
    Be centered on your grace,
That living life within your law,
    We soon shall see your face.

Psalm 19 begins celebrating the glory of God in creation, and then shifts, midpoint, to praising God for the gift of the Law — the two ways God has made himself known to people. It concludes with a double petition: to be cleansed of hidden faults and kept from presumptuous sins and their power to dominate life, especially sins of the mouth. It was from verse 11 that John Calvin developed his theology of the third use of the law: to lead us into righteous living.

Psalm 20

11.11.11.11
FOUNDATION, GORDON

The Lord answer you in your days of distress!
May God come from Zion your troubles to bless.
May God send you help, give you strength for your needs,
Rememb'ring your off'rings and merciful deeds.

The Lord grant to you the desires of your heart;
Your hopes and your plans be success from the start.
May God give you vict'ry, and fill you with joy,
God's name on your banners as forth you deploy.

I know God's anointed is heard by the Lord,
Who answers from heav'n with victorious reward.
Though some place great trust in their weapons of war,
The Lord is our trust and our pride evermore.

All those who take pride in the chariot and horse
Will fall in their struggles, be lacking in force.
But we shall arise, and upright we shall stand,
Held firm by the Lord God's victorious right hand.

P salm 20 initially seems addressed to anyone. It is an intercessory blessing: "The Lord answer you in the day of trouble; the name of the God
of Jacob protect you! May God give you support from Zion, remembering
your sacrifices and burnt offerings. May God grant you your heart's desire,
fulfill all your plans, and give you victory when you set up your banner in
God's name." Only in verse 6 does it become clear that this is ultimately
addressed to the king, "the anointed of the Lord." Where other monarchs
take pride in their chariots and horses, the king is reminded that our pride is
in the name of the Lord our God. Others will collapse and fall, but we shall
rise and stand upright. It ends with one final petition: "Save us, O Lord!

Deliver us," as it continues with its intercessions for the king. But it can also be read as, "Answer us, O King (a reference to God's sovereignty), when we call." Though originally a royal psalm, it is to be prayed in confidence by all of God's anointed.

29

Psalm 22

Verses 1–15, 19–20

7.7.7.7.7.7

REDHEAD NO. 76, CHRIST WHOSE GLORY FILLS THE SKY

Why, Lord, have you turned aside?
   Why have you forsaken me?
Why are you so far away,
   Silent to my anguished plea?
Day and night I call for help;
   Why do you not answer me?

You are Isr'el's Holy One,
   Seated on a throne of praise.
Unto you our people called,
   Trusting you in worst of days.
You delivered them from shame,
   For you are the One who saves.

Scorned by others and despised,
   I am less than human now.
All who see me laugh and jeer.
   Mockingly they scorn my vow:
"On the Lord you placed your trust,
   Where is God to save you now?"

Yet you brought me from the womb,
   Safe unto my mother's breast.
You have always been my God,
   Source of life and place of rest.
Trouble now surrounds me, Lord.
   Do not leave me in this test.

Raving lions, vicious bulls,
   Threaten and encircle me.
All my bones are out of joint;

I am weak and cannot flee.
Fear has turned my heart to wax,
    While they stare and gloat at me.

Come, Lord, do not stay away;
    Clearly hear my urgent plea.
Scatter those who seek my life;
    From their power set me free.
Come now, Lord, and rescue me;
    Save me from their treachery.

Verses 22–31

CMD

ELLACOMBE, HUNTSVILLE, FOREST GREEN

Amid the thronging worshipers,
    The living Lord I bless;
Before my people, gathered here,
    God's name will I confess.
Come sing with all who fear the Lord,
    You children of God's grace;
With reverence sound all glory forth,
    And bow before God's face.

The burden of the sorrowful,
    The Lord will not despise;
God has not turned from those who mourn,
    But listens to their cries.
Such goodness makes me join the throng,
    Where saints this praise proclaim,
And there will I fulfill my vows,
    With those who fear God's name.

You feed with good the humble ones,
    And satisfy the meek,
And they shall live and praise you, Lord,

Who for your mercy seek.
The ends of all the earth take thought,
   The nations seek you, Lord.
They worship you, the Sovereign One,
   In earth and heav'n adored.

Before you, Lord, the proud shall bow,
   The haughty with their trust.
They cannot keep themselves alive,
   They too return to dust.
But you, Lord, dwell beyond all time,
   Deliv'rence to proclaim,
To generations yet unborn,
   Who shall confess your name.

32

Stanzas 1–3 initially appeared in the 1912 Psalter as a versification of Psalm 22 under the title "Amid the Thronging Worshippers" in Tudor English, using "Jehovah" for "the Lord" and "Brethren" for people. In 1984, the Psalter Task Force of the PCUSA asked me to modify stanzas 1–3 using inclusive language and to write a new final stanza. In the 1912 Psalter it is sung to the tune BOVINA C.M.D.

Verses 25–31
CMD

Come, bless with me the living Lord,
   The reason for my praise.
Join in my vow of gratitude;
   Come, bless God's saving ways.
The poor shall eat, they shall be filled;
   They too will praise you, Lord;
O may their hearts forever live,
   And praise with one accord.

Remember, nations of the earth,
   And turn unto the Lord.

Come, fam'lies from across the world,
    Your worship to afford.
For royal power is the Lord's;
    Almighty is God's hand.
Dominion is the Lord's alone,
    Who rules o'er every land.

Before you shall the prosperous bow;
    All mortals and their trust.
They cannot keep themselves alive;
    They soon return to dust.
But you, Lord, dwell beyond all time,
    Deliv'rance to proclaim,
To generations yet unborn,
    Who shall confess your name.

Psalm 22 is the best-known lament in the Psalter, primarily because it contains the words that are on the lips of Jesus hanging on the cross and it is all but prophetic concerning what takes place there. It is a lengthy plea for help that describes the psalmist's troubles. Day and night he calls for help with no answer. Yet, God is the Holy One enthroned on the praises of Israel; the One his ancestors trusted and he delivered them. But the psalmist does not ask on the basis of his own righteousness. He is but a worm, not human, and scorned by others who despise and mock him. "Commit your cause to the Lord; let him deliver" is repeated in the passion (Matt. 27:43) with the chief priests, scribes, and Pharisees using these words to mock Jesus in his dying. In the midst of suffering, the psalmist remembers that God has cared for him since his birth and from that time the Lord has been his God. Again he pleads, "Do not be far from me, for trouble is near and there is no one to help." Vivid language follows to describe the psalmist's condition: surrounded by strong and destructive bulls, poured out like water, a heart melted like wax, bones out of joint, mouth dried like a potsherd, and his tongue cleaving to his jaw. The psalmist understands this as God's judgment against him: "you lay me in the dust of death," circled by dogs ready to devour his flesh. His enemies likewise stare and gloat over his suffering and divide his clothing among them by casting lots — another image Matthew includes at the cross. After one final plea for the Lord's presence and aid to save him from the power of the dog and the mouth of the lion, suddenly there is a shift in the second half of verse 21: "From the horns of the wild oxen you have rescued me." God has acted. The rest of the psalm is one of praise to God for not hiding his face, for answering and for coming to the psalmist in his distress. The psalm is exultant and filled with promises to testify to the Lord's goodness among his brothers and sisters in the midst of the congregation. His rescue is such that all the ends of the earth shall remember and turn to the Lord; and all the families of the nations shall worship him. For dominion belongs to the Lord, and he rules over the nations. Even those yet unborn will be told about the Lord and proclaim him. It is easy to see why the infant church found in this psalm prophetic witness to Jesus's passion, death, resurrection, and eternal rule, and how its influence found its way into the passion narratives.

Psalm 23

8.7.8.7
To be sung to ST. COLUMBA

You are my shepherd, and my Lord;
    In rich green land you nourish.
I have no need you will not fill;
    In you my days shall flourish.

Beside a calm, deep-running stream,
    You lead me for renewing.
My soul refreshed, you lead me on,
    Your righteous work pursuing.

And when I walk through death's despair,
    With all its pain and grieving,
I fear no evil; you are there,
    To bring me your own healing.

In view of all my enemies,
    You set before me daily
A table filled with food for life;
    You nourish me in safety.

Your holy oil anoints my head,
    A pledge forgotten never.
My cup is filled beyond its brim
    To quench my thirst forever.

So shall your mercy and your good
    O'ershadow all my living,
And I shall dwell within your house,
    For time that knows no ending.

Psalm 23 is the best known of all the psalms, and perhaps the most intimate in the entire Psalter, portraying the Lord as a shepherd who cares for us, as a shepherd cares for his sheep — and does so in such a way that the sheep has no wants. (The word for sheep is singular — this is not a flock!) The Lord leads to verdant pasture and to still water. Sheep are infamously skittish, and the noise of running water is problematic. But still water is safe to drink. Now the image turns even more personal: he restores my "soul" — the word in Hebrew means "inner being," "self," or "sense of being alive and strong." He leads in right paths, for the sake of his own name. It is God being true to God's own nature. Remember that shepherds in the ancient Near East did not follow sheep, but walked out ahead of them, their voices the sign for the sheep to follow. The Lord leads us always in the right way by his word. All of this is an affirmation of the intimate care and concern each of us can expect from the Lord. Even in the darkest valleys and bleakest times of life, there is no need to fear because the Lord is there, present, ready to help. The crook and walking staff that are so crucial to the shepherd's work give the psalmist security and comfort. God sets a table — providing all that is needed. Even in the presence of our enemies, we can be so assured and confident in God's care that we have the leisure to eat at a well-set table. The Lord not only feeds us, he anoints our heads in blessing and fills our cups beyond the brim. "Goodness and mercy" are God's gifts, and they will not simply be given to us, but actually *pursue us* all the days of our lives. "I shall dwell in the house of the Lord my whole life long" is both a vow and a confession, as the reference is twofold. First, it is a reference to the temple, where God was believed to live, but more, it is a vow expressing commitment to daily intimacy with God, regardless of where one might be. The word the King James Version translated as "forever" means "my whole life long," as most footnotes now indicate. It is rendered in other translations: "through length of days," or "as long as I live." But following Jesus's resurrection and his promises, "forever" is absolutely appropriate as well. Though this psalm is most often associated with funerals or memorial services, it is really an affirmation of God's daily care. This is also the psalm that lies behind Jesus's describing himself as the "Good Shepherd" (John 10:11–18). But he not only cares for his sheep, he actually lays down his life for them.

Psalm 24

11.11.11.11
FOUNDATION, JOANNA *(St. Denio)*

The earth is yours, Lord, and the fullness of all,
The world and its people, the great and the small.
For you have established all things on the earth,
All matter, all creatures in this universe.

And who shall ascend to the hill of the Lord,
To stand in God's presence and worship afford?
All those with clean hands and all those with pure hearts
Who give not their living to do evil's arts.

All these will be blest by the hand of the Lord;
Salvation and honor are their sure reward.
How blest are the ones who in life seek your face,
Who long for your presence to sing of your grace.

Then lift up your gates now, come open your doors;
The King of all ages now comes to these shores.
And who is this Royal One, coming to reign?
The King of all glory; "the Lord" is God's name.

Psalm 24 is a creation psalm joined to a liturgy of entrance to the temple to praise God, but also to remind worshipers that the qualification for being in God's presence is clean hands and a pure heart, not sacrifice. It begins less in praise than simply acknowledgment that the Lord possesses all that is and is sovereign over it. The Lord not only possesses the earth, but also founded it on the primordial sea and rivers, which according to the cosmology of that day rested beneath the earth. Then the temple entrance liturgy is invoked. Who shall ascend the hill of the Lord (Mt. Zion, where the temple is located)? Who shall stand in God's holy place? Those whose lives are moral, who avoid falsehood and do not swear deceitfully; these will receive blessing from the Lord. Finally, the temple doors are commanded to open so that the King of Glory — the Lord — might enter and take his rightful place. Who is the King of Glory? The Lord is the King of Glory, who is described as both warrior, strong and mighty in battle, and the Sovereign and Lord of all the heavenly hosts.

Psalm 25

Verses 1–10

LM

PARK STREET

Lord, unto you we lift our hearts;
    We place our trust in your own name.
Keep us secure against all foes;
    Lord, let us never fall to shame.
    Lord, let us never fall to shame.

Make us to know your paths, O Lord;
    Teach us to walk in your own ways.
So bind our hearts to your own heart,
    That we may serve you all our days.
    That we may serve you all our days.

Think not, O Lord, upon our sin,
    Nor look upon our childish ways.
But filled with mercy, love, and grace,
    Remember us beyond our days.
    Remember us beyond our days.

To all who keep your covenant,
    You give your health and steadfast love.
You lead the humble in your paths,
    And give them wisdom from above.
    And give them wisdom from above.

Psalm 25 is a prayer in which the psalmist pleads for God's protection, guidance, mercy, instruction, pardon, and grace. A wisdom psalm, it is acrostic in structure — the first word of each line beginning with a descending letter of the Hebrew alphabet — and repeats the convictions that those who wait upon the Lord and who walk in God's ways (Torah) will never be put to shame, while the wantonly treacherous will end in disgrace and defeat. Seeking for the wisdom ever to know God's ways, the psalmist asks to be led in God's truth and taught God's ways. He pleads for God's mercy and steadfast love and asks that the sins of his youth be forgotten. He blesses the Lord as good and upright, who instructs sinners and leads the humble in the paths of steadfast love and faithfulness. In the midst of many foes he asks that they not prevail or put him to shame, for he has taken refuge in the Lord. May that integrity and uprightness be a source of strength and preservation as he waits on God. Finally, the scope of this petition is expanded beyond personal concerns to pray that God will redeem all Israel out of its troubles.

Psalm 26

7.6.7.6 D

BOUNDLESS MERCY, ST. KEVIN, AVE VIRGO VERGINUM *(preferred tune)*

Vindicate me now, O Lord;
    You I trust completely.
Prove me, test my heart, and see
    How I walk uprightly.
I have followed you in truth,
    Trusting in your power.
Steadfast is your love, O Lord,
    Constant every hour.

In the wicked and the false,
    I have not confided.
With the evil and the base,
    I have not resided.
With clean hands I come to you,
    Here, before your altar,
Singing songs of thanks and praise,
    Words of awe and wonder.

How I love your house, O Lord;
    Wondrous is your glory!
Save me from the sinners' fate,
    And their tangled story.
Let me stand on level ground,
    In your congregation,
And I'll bless your name once more,
    With great celebration.

Psalm 26 could easily have been written by Job. It pleads for vindication while insisting on one's own integrity. The psalmist has trusted in the Lord with unwavering devotion. If there is any doubt of that on God's part, then prove her, try her, test her heart and mind. She walks faithfully, trusting in God's steadfast love. She continues to make her point: she does not sit with the worthless or consort with hypocrites; she hates the company of evildoers and shuns the wicked. In innocence she washes her hands, cleansing herself in preparation for offering temple sacrifice, and circles the altar singing songs of thanksgiving and praise (rather than penitence seeking forgiveness). How she loves being there and doing that! And so she asks that she not be swept away with sinners, the bloodthirsty whose hands are filled with evil and bribes. As for her, she walks in integrity and so pleads for God's gracious redemption. Standing in the midst of the congregation, she continues to bless the Lord.

Psalm 27

8.7.8.7 D

IN BABILON, FABEN, ABBOT'S LEIGH, ELLESDIE, BLAENHAFREN,
BLAENWERN *(preferred tune)*

Lord, my light and my salvation,
    Whom in life have I to fear?
You my stronghold, my foundation,
    When life's darkness closes near.
When the wicked rise against me,
    Filled with slander and with hate,
You rise up to make them stumble.
    Lord, my light, on you I wait.

Though a host encamp against me,
    Yet, my heart shall not be moved.
Though their warriors rise to slay me,
    Still my trust in you is proved.
This one thing will I seek after:
    Let me dwell in your accord.
Grant me life within your presence;
    Let me see your beauty, Lord.

In the day of pain and trouble
    You will hide me in your tent.
You my constant rock and shelter,
    Foil my enemies' intent.
When you lift me high above them,
    Can I help but shout your praise?
Joyful here within your presence,
    I will bless you all my days.

If my father or my mother
    Ever should abandon me,
You will not leave me forsaken;
    You give ear to every plea.

Teach me, Lord, your ways most holy;
    Lead me on your level path.
Keep me from my false accusers;
    Shield me from their violent wrath.

I shall see the Lord's own goodness
    In my life and in this land.
Trust the Lord, wait on God's kindness;
    Let your heart with courage stand.
Wait upon the Lord, be steadfast;
    Wait in confidence and cheer.
You shall see the Lord's salvation;
    You will know the Lord is near.

Psalm 27 expresses confidence in the presence of the Lord and does so in triumphal language. "The Lord is my light and my salvation, whom then shall I fear?" The psalmist's enemies — "evildoers," adversaries, foes — all shall stumble and fall because of the Lord's care. "Even though an army encamps against me, yet, my heart shall not fear." The imagery of a fearful heart is so true to life when anxiety hits. Now the psalm turns more reflective: "One thing have I asked of the Lord and that will I seek after: to dwell in the house of the Lord all the days of my life, to behold the beauty of the Lord and to inquire in his temple." The psalmist affirms (and perhaps even recalls) God's sheltering care in the day of trouble and again turns victorious and exultant with promises of sacrifice, shouts of joy, and songs (psalms) and melodies to the Lord. Notice the kind of face-to-face intimacy of relationship that is being sought as the psalmist pleads not to be turned aside. This includes the extraordinary confession, "Though my mother and father forsake me, the Lord will not, but will take me up." There follows the request to be taught the Lord's ways and to be led on a level path (who of us does not want life without its ups and downs?). The psalm ends with the affirmation, "I believe I shall see the goodness of the Lord in the land of the living," followed by "Wait for the Lord, be strong, let your heart take courage. Wait for the Lord." This last phrase, in one or another form, appears some fourteen times in the Old Testament, better than a third of them in the Psalter.

Psalm 29

CMD

KINGSFOLD, HALIFAX *(preferred tune)*

Ascribe to God both strength and pow'r;
    Come worship in God's name.
The universe proclaims our Lord;
    Must we not do the same?
God's voice rolls through heav'n and sea,
    And thunders o'er the land.
This voice is full of majesty,
    More mighty than the wind.

The trees are stripped, the leaves are shred;
    God makes the forest bare.
There is no force upon the earth
    That can with God compare.
The wilderness is God's domain,
    It too shakes at that voice.
Its shifting sand and barren space
    Sing praises and rejoice.

God sits enthroned above the flood;
    Let all creation sing.
Great strength and peace abide with those
    Who worship God as King.
The Lord is sovereign for all time,
    Majestic is God's name.
The whole creation sings God's praise;
    Must we not do the same?

P salm 29 appears to be the appropriation of a Canaanite hymn to Baal, who was believed to be a warrior god whose voice was heard in the thunder and other aspects of the storm. However, here, Israel has taken all the features of the storm and attributed them to the voice of the Lord. It thunders, is sovereign over the waters, is powerful and full of majesty. Its lightning and wind break the cedars of Lebanon, and its flashes cause the land to skip like a calf and a young wild ox. The Lord's voice sends flames of fire that shake the wilderness. Its wind causes the oaks to whirl and it strips the forest bare. And to all of this, the heavenly beings are called to ascribe to God's name "Glory, strength, and holy splendor." As the storm continues to break forth, terrifying others, those in the temple shout "Glory!" The psalm concludes by remembering that the Lord is God of the storm, and the flood, and sits enthroned as King forever, giving strength to his people. It ends with a prayer for God's blessing of peace. Any who have come through a hurricane or other great storm have some sense of the majesty and power of the sea, flood, and wind. Remembering that God is Lord of all of this,

how can we not join in shouting "Glory!"

Psalm 30

CMD

ELLACOMBE

I will extol your name, O Lord,
  For you have rescued me.
You have not let my foes rejoice;
  You give me victory.
O Lord, my God, I cried for help;
  You saved me from the pit,
Restoring me to daily life,
  Among the saints to sit.

Come sing to God, O living saints,
  Sing praises to God's name.
God's anger is not permanent;
  God's love will never wane.
Though tears may tarry for the night,
  With sighs of deepest pain,
Yet joy comes with the morning sun,
  A peace that is not vain.

In my success I felt secure;
  How good you've been to me.
I said that this was my own work,
  Ascribing all to me.
But when you turned aside your face,
  My life was filled with fears.
I begged for help; to you I cried
  With loud and bitter tears.

What good is gained by my disgrace,
  What profit in defeat?
My grave cannot confess your name,
  Nor praise for you repeat.

Now hear, O Lord, my plaintive cry;
　　Be merciful to me.
Accept my longing heart's request,
　　And from death set me free.

You change my grief to joy-filled dance;
　　My sorrows you destroy.
In faithfulness you hear my cry,
　　And fill my life with joy.
And so to you my heart shall sing,
　　My voice your goodness raise.
You are my God, for evermore;
　　My life shall sing your praise.

Psalm 30 offers praise to God for recovery from a grave illness. The Lord has "drawn him up." The "foes" are not necessarily classic enemies, but simply those who, like Job's friends, insisted that his illness was the result of his own sin. God has not let them rejoice over him. Rather, he cried to the Lord and the Lord responded, bringing him up from the land of the dead and the pit of death. Consequently, the psalm calls on all to sing praise to the Lord and give thanks to his holy name. He then recalls the error of his previous ways: in his prosperity he had thought himself unmovable, and in spite of this, the Lord's favor had enabled him to stand firm like a mountain. But then the Lord looked away, hid his face, and suddenly the psalmist was faced with the error of his ways. Yet he cried out to the Lord: "What profit is there in my death; can I praise God from the grave?" And so, he cries, "Hear, O Lord, be gracious to me and be my helper." He tells us that God responded and turned his mourning into dancing, his lament into a song of praise, removing his sackcloth and girding him with joy and gladness so that his soul could sing praises to the Lord forever. He will not again be presumptuous, but will give thanks and praise to God for the goodness of life forever.

Psalm 31

Verses 1–3, 15–16
9.8.9.8
ST. CLEMENT

In you, O Lord, I seek my refuge;
    Let me not e'er be put to shame.
In righteousness be my deliverer;
    I wait and trust in your strong name.

Incline your ear to all my pleading;
    My comfort, help, and safety be.
My fortress strong, my rock and refuge,
    For your name's sake, come rescue me.

My times are in your hand's safe keeping;
    From foes, Lord, come and set me free.
In steadfast love now save your servant;
    Come, let your face now shine on me.

Verses 9–16
CMD
HALIFAX

Be gracious to me, O my Lord,
    For I am in distress.
My body wastes away in grief,
    My soul and eyes bereft.
My life is lost in sorrow's groans;
    My years are but a sigh.
My strength is sapped by misery;
    My bones in weakness cry.

I am the scorn of every foe,
    A horror to my friends,
An object of the deepest dread
    To those I barely know.
All flee from me as if I'm dead,
    A broken, useless thing.
They whisper terrifying plots
    And for my life they scheme.

Yet I will trust in you, O Lord;
    "You are my God," I say.
My time and life are in your hands;
    Deliver me, I pray.
So let your face upon me shine;
    You are my only stay.
In steadfast love, Lord, rescue me;
    Give life to me this day.

P salm 31 is both petition and praise, and though identified as a "Psalm of David," is a composite, echoing phrases from other well-known psalms (Pss. 4:1; 18:19; 27:14; 33:18, 22; 38:15; 69:3; 71:1–3; 115:17; 118:5). It begins with a confession of faith: "In you, O Lord, I seek refuge; do not let me ever be put to shame" — virtually identical with 71:1–3. God is to respond, not because of the psalmist's virtue, but for God's own name's sake — to preserve God's reputation! Verse 3 begins to list the reasons for praise and trust: you are my rock, fortress, guide, and redeemer. It then moves to an expression of trust, confessing that God has placed him "in a broad place." (See Pss. 18:19 and 118:5.) It is followed by a plea for deliverance, followed by an exhortation to wait for the Lord. (See Ps. 27:14.) Verse 5 appears on the lips of Jesus as he is dying (Luke 23:46). Images and phrases from other psalter sources abound: "Let your face shine upon me." "Do not let me be put to shame, O Lord." "Blessed be the Lord who has shown his steadfast love to me." It ends with wisdom's counsel: "The Lord preserves the faithful, but abundantly repays the one who acts haughtily." Finally, to the familiar "all you who wait for the Lord," it adds the injunction, "Be strong, and let your heart take courage."

Psalm 32

7.6.7.6 D

EWING, MUNICH

How blest are those whose great sin
    Has freely been forgiv'n,
Whose guilt is wholly covered
    Before the sight of heav'n.
Blest those to whom our Lord God
    Will not impute their sin,
Whose guilt has been forgiven,
    Whose heart is true again.

While I kept guilty silence,
    My strength was spent with grief.
Your hand was heavy on me;
    My life found no relief.
But when I made confession,
    And hid no sin from you,
When I revealed my own guilt,
    You gave me life anew.

So let the godly seek you,
    When troubling times are near.
No whelming floods shall reach them,
    Nor cause their hearts to fear.
In you, O Lord, I hide me;
    You save me from all ill,
And songs of your salvation
    My heart with rapture fill.

"I graciously will teach you,
    The way that you should go,
And with my eye upon you,

My counsel you shall know.
But be not then unruly,
 Or slow to understand.
Be not perverse, but willing,
 To heed my wise command."

The sorrows of the wicked
 In number shall abound,
But those who trust our own God,
 Great mercy shall surround.
Then in the Lord be joyful;
 In song lift up your voice.
Be glad in God, you righteous;
 Rejoice, O saints, rejoice.

Stanzas 1–3, The Psalter, 1912, alt., Fred R. Anderson; stanzas 4–5, Fred R. Anderson

Psalm 32 is a wisdom psalm in which the psalmist gives thanks for the gift of forgiveness. "Happy are those whose sin is covered." He acknowledges that while he kept silent about his sin, he wasted away, for the Lord's hand was heavy upon him, and his strength was dried up as the heat of summer dries all things. But when he acknowledged his sin, when he no longer hid it but confessed it, the Lord forgave him his guilt. The psalmist then instructs all who are faithful to offer such prayers of confession, promising that in a time of distress and the rush of many waters, these will not reach or overwhelm them. Again, addressing the Lord, he confesses that God is his hiding place, the One who preserves him from trouble and surrounds him with glad cries of deliverance. The psalm now turns to addressing others, instructing them in the way they should go: "Do not be like a horse or a mule, without understanding, whose temper must be curbed with bit and bridle, else it will not stay near." It concludes with one final double affirmation: "Many are the torments of the wicked, but steadfast love surrounds those who trust in the Lord. Therefore be glad in the Lord and rejoice, O righteous, and shout for joy, all you upright in heart."

Psalm 33

Verses 1–12

10.9.10.9.9.8

To be sung to BRING A TORCH

Come, rejoice in the Lord, O you righteous!
For glad praises befit the upright.
Praise the Lord with the sound of the lyre,
For the Lord's word and works are upright.
Love, faith, justice are God's own making.
Earth is full of God's steadfast love.

By your word, Lord, the worlds were created;
By your breath all the hosts were designed.
Seas and rivers you gathered together,
Holding their deeps as in a storehouse.
Your word spoke and they were created.
Let all things stand in awe of God.

Lord, you frustrate the wisdom of nations,
Bring the plans of their people to naught.
For your counsel to all generations
Strengthens the heart, is sure forever.
Glad the nation that you have chosen,
Blest the people who call you Lord.

Verses 18–22

8.7.8.7

CHARLESTON, KINGDOM

Lord, you watch o'er all who love you,
    Trusting in your steadfast care.
And you save from death's destruction,
    Giving hope in life's despair.

You, our only sure protection,
    And our hope in all life's needs.
Trusting in your name and goodness
    Brings us joy in all our deeds.

May your constant love and mercy
    Be with us, forever, Lord.
As in hope and trust we serve you,
    May your name be long adored.

Psalm 33 asks about the identifying mark of the upright — praise, praise that makes melody to the Lord on the ten-stringed harp, and sings to him new songs of praise filled with loud shouts of joy. After three verses calling the assembly to praise the Lord, the reasons for such praise are identified. The word of the Lord is upright; all his works are done in faithfulness. He loves righteousness and justice. The earth is filled with his steadfast love. Verses 6–9 form the foundation of creation theology: "By the word of the Lord the heavens were made. . . ." God spoke and creation came into being. These verses had strong influence on the creation narrative in Genesis 1. God's "counsel" is superior to all others' — happy is the nation whose God is the Lord. God's eye is all-seeing. Kings are not saved by great armies or warriors by their strength. The war horse is a vain hope for victory. Rather, the eye of the Lord is on those who fear him, those who hope in his steadfast love and look to him to deliver their souls from death. The psalm ends with the recurring theme and commitment to wait for the Lord who is both help and shield. As they wait, their hearts are glad because they trust in God's holy name. The psalm ends with a final plea: "Let your steadfast love, O Lord, be upon us, even as we hope in you."

Psalm 34

Verses 1–10, 22

7.6.7.6 D

BOUNDLESS MERCY, TEMPUS ADEST FLORIDUM

We will always bless you, Lord,
   In all times and places.
We will thank and laud your name;
   We will sing your praises.
Come, afflicted, come, oppressed;
   God will heal your sadness.
Join with us and sing this song;
   God will give you gladness.

Lord, our God, you heard our prayer,
   And from fear you freed us.
In our hunger we cried out;
   You drew near to feed us.
All the homeless come to you,
   Safe and Sturdy Shelter.
Lost and troubled seek your face,
   Sure and Constant Helper.

When the helpless call on God,
   Angels come descending.
In their shelt'ring wings is peace,
   Strength to calm all trembling.
Blest are those who come to you,
   Good and Sure Defender.
Taste and see, the Lord is good,
   Source of life and splendor.

Though young lions suffer want,
   And are filled with hunger,
Those who seek the Lord receive
   Good things without number.

You redeem your servants' lives;
    Lord, you are salvation.
None whose refuge is the Lord
    Shall know condemnation.

P salm 34 is attributed to David, when he feigned madness before the Philistine king Abimelech so that the king drove him out, allowing David to escape. It is a wisdom psalm that focuses on God's goodness. The psalm is built on an acrostic pattern, each new section beginning with a word that begins with the successive letter of the Hebrew alphabet. It uses a number of parallelisms, the first phrase making a statement that the second phrase repeats with different language: "I will bless the Lord at all times; his praise shall be continually in my mouth." "O magnify the Lord with me, and let us exalt his name together." "Taste and see that the Lord is good; happy are those who take refuge in him." These, of course, have been solidly incorporated in the liturgical language of the church, as the Psalter was its first prayerbook. The psalm is testimonial through and through: "I sought the Lord, and he answered me. . . . Look to him, and be radiant. . . . This poor soul cried, and was heard by the Lord." The young are then summoned to listen and learn the fear of the Lord and what it means for their lives. "The Lord is near to the brokenhearted, and saves the crushed in spirit. Many are the afflictions of the righteous, but the Lord rescues them from them all. . . . The Lord redeems the life of his servants; none of those who take refuge in him will be condemned."

Psalm 36

Verses 5–10
CMD
KINGSFOLD, HALIFAX *(preferred tune)*

Your steadfast love, O living Lord,
    Fills all the worlds that are.
Your faithfulness exceeds the heav'ns
    Beyond the farthest star.
Your righteousness is strong and firm,
    Like mountains it is sure.
Your judgments are so right and sound;
    Your creatures rest secure.

"How precious is your steadfast love,"
    The whole creation sings.
A refuge sure is found beneath
    The shadow of your wings.
Within their shelter shines true light;
    Life's fountain ever flows
with drink from rivers of delight,
    And rest from all life's woes.

Pour out your steadfast love, O Lord,
    On all who know your name.
Give health and strength and righteousness
    To each one that you claim.
The gifts of your abundant house
    To each of us now send,
That we may feast upon your love,
    Salvation without end.

Psalm 36 reflects on the difference between those who take pride in their transgressions and those who trust in the loving kindness of the

Lord. It begins addressing the capacity for wickedness deep within the human heart. Is it the psalmist speaking, reflecting on the ways of the wicked, or is it transgression itself speaking to the wicked, deep in their hearts? Both are possible. Yes, the wicked have no fear of God. There is no end to the way they flatter themselves in their own eyes, thinking that their iniquity is hidden. They have ceased to live wisely and spend their time plotting mischief and embracing evil rather than rejecting it. Suddenly, in contrast, as if to keep one from despair, the psalmist turns to praise for the Lord's steadfast love, which extends to the heavens. God's righteousness is like the mighty mountains, God's judgments like the great deep. The Lord saves humans and animals alike. The psalm lauds the preciousness of God's steadfast love and confesses that all take refuge in the shadow of God's wings. It goes on to speak of the abundance and goodness of God's house, where God gives

drink from the river of delights. God is the fountain of life; in his light we see light. The prayer concludes by asking for God's continued steadfast love to those who know him. As for the arrogant with whom this psalm began, do not let their foot tread on him; do not let the hand of the wicked drive him away. Rather, let the Lord continue his salvation. As for evildoers, let them lie prostrate, thrust down, unable to rise.

Psalm 37

Verses 1–11, 39–40
CMD
MINERVA

Fret not yourself with wickedness,
　　Nor those who through it gain.
As grass dries up and flowers fade,
　　Their end will be the same.
But trust the Lord and seek the good,
　　Live on the land in praise.
With everything delight in God,
　　Who guards us all our days.

Commit yourself to God in trust,
　　The Lord will be your stay,
To vindicate you and your cause,
　　As light brings forth the day.
Be still before the Lord and wait,
　　Abandon fretful fear
Of all who prosper from the wrong
　　They do from year to year.

Refrain from anger and from wrath;
　　These too are evil's way.
One day they too shall disappear,
　　As patience wins the day.
And then the wicked will be gone,
　　And all their trouble cease.
While those of humble faith and trust
　　Will live in endless peace.

Salvation is the Lord's own gift,
　　To those who walk God's way.

In times of trouble or distress,
    The Lord is strength and stay.
The Lord is refuge, help, and strength,
    When wicked seek our shame.
Sure help and rescue come to all
    Who call upon God's name.

P salm 37:1–11, 39–40 is an instruction acrostic from the wisdom tradition that counsels, "Do not fret because of the wicked; do not be envious of wrongdoers, for they will soon fade like the grass and wither like the green herb. Trust in the Lord, and do good; so you will live in the land, and enjoy security." With this and other such injunctions the psalm encourages patient trust in the Lord in the face of the prosperity of the wicked. It is from the Yahwist tradition, with the name "Lord" used for God again and again, constantly exhorting: "Trust in the Lord." Its purpose is to instruct and encourage people in the face of watching the wicked prosper. "Commit your way to the Lord; trust in him, and he will act." "Be still before the Lord, and patiently wait for him." Abandon anger, wrath, and fretting, for they only lead to doing evil. Remember, the evildoers will be cut off while the Lord knows the days of the blameless, whose heritage will abide forever. In a little while, you will look for the wicked but find that "they are no more." The psalm then reflects on the ways of the wicked, continuing to affirm that the blameless will not be put to shame. Its acrostic structure functions to contrast the wicked from the righteous in a series of proverbs, concluding, "Wait for the Lord, and keep his ways, and he will exalt you to inherit the land; you will look on the destruction of the wicked." The salvation of the righteous is from the Lord; he is their refuge in time of trouble. The Lord helps them and rescues them; he rescues them from the wicked and saves them because they take refuge in him.

Psalm 40

CMD

HALIFAX

In patience, Lord, I waited long
    For you to hear my cry.
You heard my voice and answered me;
    On you I can rely.
You drew me from the deadly pit,
    And made my life secure.
You put a new song in my mouth,
    Praise that will long endure.

How blest are those who trust in you,
    When others serve false gods.
You multiply your wondrous deeds
    Against all worldly odds.
Were I to try to speak of them,
    My words would be too frail.
The goodness of your thoughts toward us
    Are gifts that never fail.

Burnt offerings and sacrifice
    Are not the gifts you seek,
But life lived out in faithfulness,
    Your law to gladly keep.
In gratitude that's unrestrained
    I speak of your great deeds.
With open heart I praise once more
    Your grace that meets all needs.

When evil and iniquity
    Descend upon my life,
Come quickly, Lord, deliver me,
    And take away the strife.

Let all who seek you find relief,
And then in one accord,
Join with this company of saints
To sing, "Great is the Lord!"

P salm 40 falls into two sections: the first a song of praise for God's deliverance in time of need, the second, a new plea for help and God's
intervention. Whereas many psalms begin describing the time and situation
of need and then turn to an expression of thanksgiving for deliverance, this
one begins confessing to God, in the midst of the great congregation, God's
saving help and salvation. Waiting patiently for the Lord never brings disap-
pointment; happy are those who place their trust in him. It is not sacrifice
or offering that the Lord desires, but an obedient life that entrusts itself to
God's care and is willing to wait. And so the psalmist waits, but not quietly!
Rather he seeks God's steadfast love and faithfulness because it has been
experienced before in similar times of trial. Confessing not only the evils
that have encompassed him, but also his own iniquities beyond number, the
psalmist asks for God's mercy as well as protection — to be saved from those
attempting to snatch life away from him; let them be put to shame. Finally,
the psalm ends with a plea that all who seek the Lord may rejoice in God's
love and salvation. Though the psalmist is poor and needy, the Lord is his
help; the Lord remembers and delivers. And so he concludes, "Do not delay,
O my God." The last five verses appear in Psalm 70 as a singular prayer for
deliverance from enemies.

Psalm 41

II.IO.II.IO
VICAR

Happy are those who with the poor have mercy;
　　In time of trouble, Lord, you are their stay.
You give them life; all people call them blessed,
　　And from their enemies you guard their way.

Lord, you sustain them when they lie in sickness,
　　And heal them of all their infirmities.
You guard against all things that would afflict them;
　　You keep them safe from all their enemies.

As for myself, I said, "O Lord, have mercy!
　　Heal me, O Lord; against you I have sinned."
My enemies, in malice, work against me
　　To spread abroad their mischief and offend.

All those who hate me whisper words of malice,
　　And they imagine that I'll surely die.
They think a deadly thing has fastened on me,
　　And I'll not rise again from where I lie.

Even my friends that I once trusted, shun me;
　　They ate my bread, but now they scorn my way.
But you, O Lord, be gracious; come and help me,
　　And raise me up that them I may repay.

By this I'll know in me you still take pleasure,
　　When my foes have not triumphed over me.
In my integrity you hold me upright,
　　And set me in your presence endlessly.

63

Blest be the Lord, the God of Israel's people,
　From everlasting to eternity.
Come shout "Amen," and bless the Lord my savior,
　"Amen!" To God sing praises endlessly.

P salm 41 expresses the conviction that those who look after the poor
will be delivered by God in the day of their own troubles. Having
said that, the psalmist pleads for God's graciousness and healing, confessing
that he has sinned against God. As he descends deeper into his illness, even
his friends are perceived to be his enemies, who he describes as whispering
hateful things against him, imagining the worst of and for him, yet coming
to his bedside with empty words. Even his most trusted friends have turned
against him, or so it seems. And so, justifying himself against charges of
complicity, he pleads to be raised up, *so that he may repay them!* By this he
will know of God's recognition of his integrity. The psalm ends with a dox-
ology, in part because it brings to a conclusion Book I of the five into which
the Psalter is divided.

Psalm 42

10.10.10.10.10
OLD 124TH

As deer long for a cool and flowing stream,
So longs my soul for you, O God of grace.
When shall I come to look upon your face?
Tears are my only food, both night and day,
While people taunt: "Where is your God?" they say.

This I remember, pouring out my soul,
How to your house I went to seek your face.
I led the throng into that holy place,
In great procession, on those festal days,
With shouts of joy and songs of thanks and praise.

Why so cast down, my soul, why such despair?
Why so bereft, disquieted within?
Hope now in God, whom I shall praise again.
My soul, cast down, remember this: be strong,
From Jordan to Mizar and Lebanon.

Deep calls to deep, your cataracts sound forth.
Your waves and billows wash o'er where I stand.
Sure steadfast love is daily your command.
Nightly your song sustains and is my prayer,
Offered to you, O God of constant care.

I say to God, my rock, "Why is this so?
Why have you looked away, forgotten me?
Why must I walk about so mournfully?"
My foes oppress, my deadly wounds they prod;
Mocking, they taunt and ask, "Where is your God?"

65

Why so cast down, my soul, why such despair?
Why so disquieted and grieved within?
Hope now in God, whom I shall praise again,
My help, my hope, when others would assail.
God's love is steadfast; it will never fail.

Psalm 42 opens the second of five sections of the Psalter, probably composed to instruct the community on how to live as it faces exile in Babylon after 587 BCE. Its plaintive longing for contact with God (note, the divine name "the Lord" is absent throughout this collection, and instead the Hebrew word for God, *Elohim*, and variations of it are used). God's presence is sought and remembered, and God's absence lamented. Has God forgotten the psalmist? Has God forgotten the people in Babylon? Why do his enemies persist with their taunts: "Where is your God?" What is the psalmist to say? Throughout the prayer, the persistent question is asked, "Why are you cast down, O my soul," as if to keep himself from falling into despair, "and why are you disquieted within me?" In answer to his own question, the psalmist offers this refrain: "Hope in God; for I shall again praise him, my help and my God." Troubles come and go, and in the midst of them God may seem distant. But remembering God's acts and support in the past, and hoping in God for the future, draws us near to God in the present through the conversation of prayer, and reveals that God is not only present, but a rock who is unchanging — present even when seeming absent — and worthy of our trust and praise.

Psalm 43

6.7.6.7 D

BOUNDLESS MERCY, ST. KEVIN

Vindicate me, O my God;
  Come, defend me quickly.
From deceitful and unjust
  Godless ones protect me.
O my refuge, why have you
  Cast me off completely?
Must I walk about in grief,
  As my foes oppress me?

Send to me your light and truth;
  Make them my example.
Let them bring me to your hill,
  And your holy temple.
Then before your altar, and
  Filled with adulation,
I will praise you with the harp,
  God of my salvation.

Why are you cast down, my soul,
  Why so sad within me?
Why disquieted and grieved,
  Troubled so completely?
Hope in God, our one true help,
  Let us seek God's favor.
I shall praise you once again,
  God, my help, my savior.

Psalm 43 is a wonderful little psalm that is a petition for God's help in times of trouble, asking for God's vindication against the ungodly ones who have behaved in deceitful and unjust ways against her. Affirming her trust in God, she asks why this has happened: "Why have you cast me off?" Then she prays, "Send out your light and your truth; let them lead me." Isn't that what we most need when besieged by the confusion of deceit and injustice all around? Once led through the treachery of injustice, she lets God's light and truth bring her to God's holy hill in Jerusalem and to God's dwelling there, the temple. There she will worship God with exceeding joy and praise him with the harp. After reaffirming her commitments to God, the psalmist turns reflective and asks herself, "Why are you cast down, O my soul, and why are you disquieted within me?" Her counsel is the universal word that continues to resound throughout scripture: "Hope in God, for I shall again praise him, my help and my God." Yes, this is a difficult time, but God is present in it as her help, and she will again be triumphant. There will come a time beyond this when she will again be filled with joy and praise.

Psalm 45

Verses 1–2, 6–9

CMD

KINGSFOLD, ELLACOMBE

My heart is filled with God's own thoughts,
    A good and wholesome theme,
About the King, God's chosen one,
    Anointed and esteemed.
My tongue is ready, like a pen,
    A listening, ready scribe,
To speak the words God speaks through me,
    To bless and to ascribe.

O King, you are our God's own choice,
    The handsomest of men.
Your mouth is filled with words of grace;
    Your lips are free from sin.
Take up your sword, O mighty one,
    Now gird it on your thigh.
Your glory and your majesty
    Are gifts from the Most High.

Your throne, O King, is God's own throne,
    Your scepter God's own rod.
Its rule is one of equity,
    The Righteousness of God.
Your rule shall be an endless reign;
    Unceasing are its days.
You love the right and hate the wrong,
    So just are all your ways.

The oil of gladness you set forth
    As God's anointed one.
Glad songs of praise surround your throne,
    For you are God's own son.
How fragrant is your presence here,
    How lovely is your face.
Your church like queens adorned in gold,
    We seek you in this place.

Verses 10–17
7.6.7.6 D
BOUNDLESS MERCY

Hear, O daughter, and reflect;
    Give your ear to hear me.
Put away your parents' house
    And your people's mem'ry.
Then the king with all his power
    Shall desire your beauty.
Since he is your sovereign lord,
    Bow to him completely.

Tyre's own will seek your help,
    Hoping for your favor,
Bring you gifts of every kind,
    Treasures you will savor
From the richest of the land,
    Their wealth to you bringing,
Giv'n to purchase your goodwill,
    Your own friendship seeking.

Gloriously you are brought forth
    From your bridal chamber,
Clothed in robes with golden thread,
    For the king's own favor.

Joined by virgins and your friends,
　　You go forth rejoicing,
Joy and gladness on your lips,
　　For this royal wedding.

For your fam'ly left behind,
　　Great shall be your offspring,
Each one ruling in the land,
　　Royal in their being.
I will make your mem'ry great,
　　Blest by generations,
Praised forever without end,
　　In true veneration.

Psalm 45 is a wedding hymn of praise for the king — "the most handsome of men" — who is about to marry. It lists his various attributes as a military leader and a defender of the right. It celebrates the divine dynasty that has been established through David, and then addresses the bride and gives her instruction on her role as the soon-to-be queen. Submission to the king and his authority will bring her great blessing. Many kings will come from this marriage, and people will celebrate the king and queen's greatness. Verse 6 is the only place in scripture where the king is addressed as God. An alternate version of the text appeared in an attempt to smooth over the blasphemy: "Your throne is a throne of God, it endures forever and ever." However, Hebrews 1:8–9 quotes this psalm in its Greek version as support for the divine nature of the Messiah. The last half of the psalm, verses 10–17, focus upon the king's bride.

Psalm 46

8.7.8.7.3.3.7
To be sung to MICHAEL

God, our help and constant refuge:
    Ever present in our need,
Though the earth be ever changing,
    Though it fall into the sea,
Rock secure, ever sure,
    Through all tumult you endure.

Holy river of God's city,
    Healing flows within your streams,
Giving strength within our crisis,
    Firm and steady like a beam.
Nations rage, wars to wage.
    Yet God's pow'r sustains each age.

God, the Lord of Hosts, is with us.
    Come, behold these mighty deeds:
Wars are ended, spears are broken;
    To God's voice the world takes heed.
Come, O Lord; break the sword.
    Bring us peace as your reward.

Living Lord of Hosts, be with us;
    Come and fill us with your pow'r.
You, the hope of all the nations,
    Be exalted in this hour.
God Most High, lest we die,
    Give us hope and hear our cry.

Psalm 46 is a communal psalm that is a source of comfort and solace as well as an affirmation of confidence and trust in God as our only refuge and strength in times of trouble. No matter the threat or crisis — even one as dire as massive earthquakes, volcanic eruptions, or the enormous tides, tsunamis, and floods created by the sea — we will not fear, for God is with us. God is not only stronger than the forces of the earth, God is in the city of his holy habitation — Jerusalem and its temple — and it shall not be moved. The nations are in an uproar, the kingdoms totter, the Lord speaks, and the earth melts. Again, the psalm repeats the affirmation that the Lord of hosts is with us; the God of Jacob is our refuge. The psalm then invites us to look upon and consider the works of God: the Lord's sovereignty over the chaotic forces of nature and his ability to silence and still warring and ravenous nations. Therefore, be still — know God! Know that God is sovereign over all things that can harm, be it the forces of nature or the brutality of humanity. More: know that the Lord of hosts is with us; the God of Jacob is our refuge. Be still and know God.

Psalm 47

8.7.8.7 D
HYMN TO JOY

Clap your hands now, all you people;
　　Shout to God with songs of mirth,
For the Lord Most High is awesome,
　　Sovereign over all the earth.
God subdued the hostile nations,
　　Putting them beneath our feet,
Chose us as a prized possession,
　　Pride of Jacob, God's own keep.

God has gone up with loud shouting,
　　With the trumpet's sound and call.
Sing aloud to God, sing praises,
　　God our monarch, Lord of all.
For our God is truly sovereign,
　　Ruling over all the earth.
Sing a psalm to praise God's glory,
　　Praises full of joy and mirth.

God, you rule o'er all the nations,
　　Sitting on your holy throne.
All the princes of the people
　　Gather there; all are your own.
God of Abraham and Sarah,
　　All earth's shields belong to you.
Thus enthroned, exalted highly,
　　Praise and honor are your due.

P salm 47 celebrates God's reign over all the earth. It is a hymn of praise that may have been used during a festival commemorating God's covenant with Israel, and calls on the people to celebrate God's ritual enthronement. It remembers how God, the Most High, is God of the gods, the awesome king over all the earth — not just Israel. Not only has God subdued the nations, God has chosen Israel as his heritage, "the pride of Jacob whom he loves." "God has gone up with a shout, the Lord with the sound of a trumpet." All are called upon to sing praise to God as king. "Our God is king of all the earth." The phrase "God has gone up with a shout" caused the church to associate this with Jesus's resurrection and ascension, while "with the sound of a trumpet" suggests this was used as part of the liturgy for *Rosh ha-Shanah*, when the ram's horn is blown to announce the new year.

Psalm 48

10.10.10.10

SURSUM CORDA

Great is the Lord and greatly to be praised,
Within the Holy City, Mount of God,
Mount Zion, city of God's greatest king.
There God has been a sure and strong defense.

The kings assembled there, they came as one,
But when they saw it, panicked and took flight.
Trembling as women caught in pangs of birth,
As when an east wind drives ships on the rocks.

As we have heard, so also we have seen,
Within your Holy City, Lord of Hosts.
It is your home, a place of holy rest;
You have established it eternally.

We think upon your steadfast love, O God,
As in your temple, here, we meditate.
Your name, O God, like praise, surrounds the earth,
Your right hand always filled with victory.

Let Zion's Mount rejoice; Judah be glad!
God's righteous judgments will sustain you still.
Come walk about the city, then proclaim,
This is our God forever, and our guide.

P salm 48 is a classic psalm of praise that celebrates the Lord's greatness and presence on Mount Zion, the site of the temple, and another name for Jerusalem, the city of God and the psalmist's joy. It is probably a pilgrim's psalm — "as we have heard, so have we seen" — and remembers God's presence in the city setting the kings of the earth to panicked flight and smashing them as the east wind drives ships against the rocks of Tarshish. Standing within the temple, the pilgrim is struck with a moment of transcendence — this is a "thin place" in life where heaven and earth overlap — and ponders God's steadfast love, proclaiming that God's praise reaches the very ends of the earth. Walk about Zion, go all around it. Count its towers, consider its ramparts. Go through its citadels so that you can tell of its greatness to future generations. Most of all, remind them that God is our God forever and ever, and will forever be our guide.

Psalm 50

Verses 1–5

CM

AZMON, CAITHNESS, ST. MAGNUS

The mighty one, the Lord, our God,
　　Speaks, summoning the world.
From dawn 'til dusk on Zion's heights
　　God's glory is unfurled.

God comes behind devouring fire,
　　With tempest all around,
And calls on heav'n and earth to hear
　　A judgment that is sound.

"Come gather here, my godly ones,
　　All you who sacrifice,
To make a covenant with me;
　　My justice shall suffice."

The heav'ns declare God's righteousness,
　　And make God's glory known,
For God looks on our ways and deeds,
　　And is their judge alone.

Verses 1–8, 22–23

CMD

FOREST GREEN, KINGSFOLD

The mighty one, the Lord, our God,
　　Speaks, summoning the world.
From dawn 'til dusk on Zion's heights
　　God's glory is unfurled.
God comes behind devouring fire,

With tempest all around,
And calls on heav'n and earth to hear
    This judgment that is sound.

"Hear, O my people," thus God speaks,
    "I now will testify.
I am your God, the Righteous One;
    My judgments do not lie.
The covenantal sacrifice
    You bring me all your days.
Not for these gifts do I rebuke,
    But for your wicked ways.

"Mark this, all who forget your God,
    Or I will tear in two,
Both you and your unfaithful ways;
    None shall deliver you.
But those whose sacrifice is thanks
    Bring honor to my name.
All those who walk in the right way
    I will not put to shame."

Verses 7–15
CM
DUNFERMLINE

"Hear, O my people, I will speak;
I am your God, the Lord.
Your burning sacrificial work
Will bring you no reward.

"No calf from you will I accept,
No goat from your own fold.
For every beast belongs to me;
The world is mine to hold.

"I do not eat the flesh of bulls,
Nor blood of goats do drink!
An offering filled with thanks and praise,
From this I will not shrink.

"So bring to me a sacrifice
Of living thanks and praise.
Bring me your vows; in all your strife
I shall sustain your days."

We call on you, O God most high,
In glory and in shame.
You hear our prayer and answer still.
We praise and bless your name.

Psalm 50 is more a prophetic sermon than a prayer. The speaker is God and the ones being addressed are those who have come to the temple to worship God through sacrifice. In essence it says that we cannot substitute sacrifice for right conduct. The psalm is structured like a lawsuit. Initially, God calls on all creation to observe as he judges his people, those who made a covenant with God by sacrifice. Judgment begins by God declaring that he has no need for food, and even if he did, all the animals of the earth are his in the first place. What God desires is a sacrifice of thanksgiving, and paying and fulfilling their vows to him. Even now God promises to deliver those who call upon him. The wicked, on the other hand, are severely rebuked. What right do they think they have by giving lip-service to God's statutes? They hate God's discipline and leave his words behind, while making friends with thieves and keeping company with adulterers. Their mouths are filled with evil, even against their own family. In God's silence they have assumed that God was like them — duplicitous, and did not care. But now God is judging them. Mark God's word or be torn apart — it is as simple as that! Those who bring God a sacrifice of thanksgiving and who walk in God's ways honor him. To these, God will show salvation.

Psalm 51

CM

CRIMOND, EVAN, PTOMEY

Have mercy on us, living Lord;
    Remember not our sin.
According to your steadfast love
    Come cleanse us from within.

Our sin and guilt are heavy, Lord,
    And evil in your sight.
Against you only have we sinned;
    Your judgment, Lord, is right.

We're born into a guilty world,
    And sinful in our ways.
So teach us wisdom in our hearts,
    And lead us all our days.

So come and purify our lives,
    Our hearts with love redeem.
Restore us to your life-filled ways;
    Come now and make us clean.

Your Spirit place within our hearts,
    That we may teach your ways,
And all the people of the earth
    Shall learn to sing your praise.

You are not pleased with sacrifice;
    It brings you no delight.
A humble spirit giv'n in love
    Is pleasing in your sight.

Rebuild your people with your love;
   Renew us every day.
With hearts renewed, in all our work,
   Our lives shall sing your praise.

Psalm 51 is a confession of sin without peer, and as appropriate today as when it was first uttered. Tradition attributes it to David, upon being challenged by his prophet, Nathan, concerning David's sin with Bathsheba and his subsequent engineering of the military murder of her husband Uriah. However, it shows marks (especially in the last two verses) of having been written later than that, after the return from exile but before the building of the Second Temple. The center of the psalm focuses on the human heart, which to the Hebrew mind is not the center of affections, but the center of one's will. In pleading for a clean heart, the supplicant expresses the conviction that, without the gift of a new and right spirit, it is not possible to remain in obedience. The human heart is prone to pride and stubbornness. And so, he pleads for God's holy spirit to sustain him — one of the few places in the Old Testament where the phrase "holy spirit" is used. But notice, it is not yet personified, but simply an expression of God's presence. The point is, even right praise is God's gift to us, motivated by God's Spirit. We cannot offer it without God's prompting. Consequently, the psalmist utters the phrase that has become a classic invitation to prayer, "O Lord, open my lips, and my mouth shall declare your praise." He then expresses the prophets' recurring conviction that rather than sacrifice, what God truly desires in each of us is an obedient heart committed to God and God's ways. Sacrifices God may or may not accept. After all, God does not need them, and since the destruction of the temple in Jerusalem, there have been none. Prayer itself has become the new form of sacrifice. And so, a heart in which stubbornness has been broken, and self-pride crushed, is a heart God will never despise or reject. The prayer ends with a plea for Zion and the rebuilding of its walls following its sack by Babylon in 587 BCE, and for the restoration of the sacrificial system.

Psalm 52

CMD

HALIFAX, SHEPHERD'S PIPES

You masters of the universe,
    Who boast of evil gain,
Who plot destruction of God's own,
    Whose treachery brings pain,
Your tongues are razor sharp, indeed,
    Filled with deceitful spin;
You speak forth evil more than truth.
    Such things you do to win.

But God will not abide your pride,
    Nor countenance your ways.
With deadly force God will reduce
    The number of your days.
From your own house you will be snatched,
    Your tent will be torn down.
God will uproot you from the land,
    And banish your renown.

With holy fear the righteous look
    As God works judgment true.
They laugh at your deceitful ways:
    Corruption through and through.
"You trusted gold instead of God,
    Sought refuge in your wealth.
Your self-reliant might has failed,
    For God has judged your stealth.

Like ageless olive trees, I stand,
    Within your house, O God.
And lift my voice in songs of praise,

Your steadfast love to laud.
In you I will forever trust,
   Because of what you've done.
Among the saints I here proclaim
   Your Name, O Holy One.

P salm 52 is less a prayer than a confession of confidence in God to protect us from those whose lying tongues are like razors and whose deceitful ways are filled with treachery, those who plot the destruction of the godly. They love evil more than good, and lying more than speaking the truth. But God will break them down forever, snatch them from their tents and uproot them from the land of the living. As that happens, the righteous will see and fear — even laugh! — at the evildoer, proclaiming that those who refuse to take refuge in God, but prefer to trust in their own riches, shall be so destroyed. The psalmist then confesses to having taken refuge in God and become like a green olive tree in the courts of the temple. (Olive trees may lose branches and limbs that wither and die, but their roots continue to produce new sprouts, giving the tree long life and making it a biblical symbol for long, abundant, even eternal life.) The psalm concludes with an expression of trust in the steadfast love of God, thanking God for what he has done and promising to proclaim God's name, for it is good. Interestingly enough, the word for God throughout this psalm is the generic *Elohim* or *El*, rather than *Yahweh*. Nonetheless, it should be fair warning to the talking heads of the media world who indulge in character assassination with their invidious speech against others in the public's view and service.

Psalm 56

8.8. 8.8. 8.8

ST. PETERSBURG, MELITA

Be gracious to me, O my God,
    For people seek to trample me.
My enemies on me have trod;
    All day they come to hamper me.
In your sure word I trust and praise;
    I find a strength that none can raze.

All day they seek to harm my cause;
    Their thoughts are aimed at evil deeds.
They watch my steps without a pause;
    They plot to trap me in my needs.
So from their malice set me free,
    And in your anger make them flee.

My tossing and my sleepless night,
    My tears and sighs are your concern.
And when I call in anguished fright,
    Your love and care again I learn.
My foes draw back and turn away.
    You, Lord, are still my strength and stay.

In you, O Lord, I place my life,
    And praise you with my every breath.
Who then can threaten me with strife,
    For you are here to save from death.
Lord, ever keep me in your sight,
    That I may live and walk in light.

P salm 56 is a hymn of praise and trust in God in the midst of persecution, and most helpful when one is being intentionally besieged by
others. It begins with a cry for help from one afflicted on all sides. He has no
one to turn to but the Lord, and does so. Asserting that having put his trust
in God there is no one to fear, the psalmist continues to lament the work of
those who assail him, pleading that God cast them out. Notice that, without
warning, the psalm ends by acknowledging deliverance. And why? So that
he can continue to walk in God's presence according to God's life-giving
light. This psalm of trust in the face of persecution is attributed to David
when he had been captured by the Philistines at Gath (1 Sam. 21:10–15). Its
central theme is: "I put my trust in you, O God, whose word I praise and
trust. What can flesh do to me?" Continually surrounded by enemies, the
psalmist recounts the turmoil, and notes that God is watching and keeping
count so as to respond on the day when called upon. And so he exclaims,
"This I know, that God is for me!" In trusting God he finds his fear removed
and his soul delivered.

Psalm 62

Verses 5–12
CMD
RESIGNATION

For God, be silent, O my soul;
    For God in stillness wait.
My savior and my only hope,
    A mighty rock that's great.
My fortress and deliverance,
    A refuge that is true.
God is my shelter and my strength;
    O Lord, I wait for you.

O people, place your trust in God;
    In faith pour out your need.
God is a refuge at all times,
    And true with all who heed.
We are but breath, illusions all,
    Each lighter than a sigh.
On riches, evil, or vain ways,
    Let not our hearts rely.

Once God has spoken, twice I've heard,
    That power belongs to God;
And steadfast is your love, O Lord,
    By this the world is awed.
You give to each what they are due,
    According to their deeds.
For God be silent, O my soul;
    God will fulfill your needs.

Psalm 62 exhorts us to wait on God, who alone is our rock and salvation, who alone can protect. This is the dominant theme of this psalm. The first half of the psalm focuses on those who scheme for rank and position; at worst, they are nothing, and at best, a lie. In the scales of balance they are lighter than a breath. Hope not in things, whether by ill or honesty gained. Hope, rather, in the Lord. Wait on the Lord in silence — a continuing theme in the psalms — who is power and loving kindness and who rewards each of us according to our deeds and fulfills all our needs.

Psalm 63

Verses 1–8
6.7.6.7.6.6.6.6
WAS FRAG ICH NACH DER WELT

O God, you are my God;
    Most earnestly I seek you.
My soul and flesh require
    Your pow'r to make my life new.
I am a famished land,
    Parched dry, like land accursed.
My voice cries out to you;
    Come, Lord, and quench my thirst.

In your most holy place,
    I've seen your pow'r and glory.
Your steadfast love excels,
    The best of human story.
My lips will praise you, Lord,
    And on you make a claim.
I'll lift my hands in praise,
    And bless your holy name.

My soul is satisfied,
    As with a feast of riches.
My mouth is filled with joy
    And now speaks forth your praises.
In watches of the night,
    Recalling every snare,
I sing with heartfelt joy,
    Of your enduring care.

For you have been my help,
    Your right hand watching o'er me.
In shadow of your wings,
    I sing with joy in safety.
I call to mind your care,
    My help and stay most true,
And with a joy-filled heart
    My soul clings onto you.

Psalm 63 blesses God for his loving kindness and mercy — better than life itself! It is attributed to David while in the Judean wilderness, remembering the joy of having been in the sanctuary and the presence of the Lord. It contains some of the most beautiful language in the psalter, texts often used in formal prayer: "O God, you are my God, earnestly will I seek you." "My soul thirsts for you in a dry and barren land," "because your love is better than life itself, my lips will speak your praise," "in the shadow of your wings I sing for joy," "my soul clings to you; your right hand supports me," and so on. Each is suitable as opening words of prayer and prepares and centers the soul for conscious contact with God. Lying on his bed the psalmist meditates on all of this, his soul clinging to God as God's right hand holds him safe. Thus, those who seek his life to destroy it will be delivered over to the power of the sword and go down into the depths of the earth; they will become jackals' prey. The psalm concludes by affirming that the king will rejoice in God. Everyone who swears by God gives God glory, while the mouths of those who speak lies will be stopped.

Psalm 65

LMD

JERUSALEM

To you, O God, great praise is due;
In Zion shall our vows be made.
O you who answer every prayer,
To you all flesh shall come for aid.
When our iniquities rise up,
You bring forgiveness for our sin.
How blest to live within your courts,
And know your goodness once again.

Your awesome deeds deliver us,
O God; salvation is your will.
You are the hope of all the earth;
Your strength and might sustain it still.
You silence all the roaring seas,
All storms and tumults, every ploy.
All stand in awe by your great signs,
As dawn and dusk both shout for joy.

You pour your blessings on the earth;
Full and abundant are your lands.
You give us grain and pastures green,
And all the bounty of your hands.
The meadows clothe themselves with flocks;
The valleys deck themselves with grain.
They sing together in great joy
To praise the wonders of your name.

Psalm 65 celebrates God's abundance as it appears on the earth; this is the God who forgives all our transgressions! This is the God who invites people into his presence to bless them. This is the God who is known to the ends of the earth — the one who makes "the dawn and the sunset shout for joy!" — what a marvelous phrase for the glory of the sunrise and sunset! The psalm blesses God for his greatness, for he is the one who answers prayer and is abundant in forgiveness. It goes on to bless God for God's lavish acts of provision: abundant rain and water for a plentiful crop of grain, the hills dripping with the fatness of the flocks. Even the pastures of the wilderness drip with such abundance. And so the psalm blesses God's deliverance as well as God's good provision and abundant blessings from the earth. All praise is due to the Lord.

Psalm 66

Verses 1–12
7.7.7.7 D
ABERYSTWYTH

Make a joyful noise to God;
All the earth God's praise proclaim.
Sing, "How awesome are your deeds!
All your foes cringe at your name,
Thus before your might they cow'r,
Knowing of your pow'r and fame.
Let all creatures every hour
Sing grand praises to your name."

Come and see what God has done;
Awesome are your deeds, O Lord;
Turning sea into dry land.
Thus we crossed with one accord.
There, with joy, we worshiped you,
You the sovereign o'er all lands.
Let the rebels not exult,
Lest they fall into your hands.

Bless our God, who keeps us whole,
Keeping firm our every step,
Testing us in smelter's fire,
Culling us within the net,
Laying burdens on our backs;
Letting nations shame our face,
Leading us through sea and fire,
Out to this abundant place.

Bless our God, who keeps us whole,
Keeping firm our every step,
Testing us in smelter's fire,
Culling us within the net,
Laying burdens on our backs;
Making nations shame our face,
Leading us through sea and fire,
Unto this abundant place.

To your house I bring my gifts,
Here I come to keep my vow,
Words I uttered when in need,
Promises that I keep now.
Here I offer you the best
Of the things you've giv'n to me,
Off'rings of the finest kind,
Sacrifices full and free.

All who fear God, come and hear
Of the things that I will tell,
How God heard my fervent plea
And my words of praise as well.
Had my heart held wickedness,
God would not have heard my voice.
Blest be God who heard my prayer;
In God's steadfast love rejoice!

Psalm 66 calls upon the entire earth to make a joyful noise and sing to the glory of God's name, telling all how awesome God is. The whole earth is called to worship God. Then all are invited to "come and see what God has done among mortals." The psalm then remembers God's acts of redemption out of Egypt and deliverance at the Red Sea. God has kept us among the living and does not allow our feet to slip. But God also tests. And so, the people have known the burdens that come with subjugation by other peoples. But, in the end, God "brought us out into a broad and spacious place." The psalmist now vows to enter the temple with burnt offerings to fulfill the promise that his lips have made, making an offering of bulls and goats. Finally, the psalmist calls on all who fear God to listen as he tells them what God has done for him. He cried aloud and extolled God, and God listened because the psalmist was innocent. Had he cherished iniquity in his heart, God would not have heard his voice. But truly, God has listened. Blessed be God, who has neither rejected his prayer nor removed his steadfast love.

Psalm 67

9.8.9.8

ST. CLEMENT

O Lord, be gracious, come and bless us,
    And on us make your face to shine.
So every people, every nation,
    May know your saving pow'r divine.

Come and be glad now, all you nations;
    Sing songs of joy with thankfulness.
Our God is judge o'er every people,
    And rules with perfect righteousness.

Let all the people come and praise you;
    Blest be your name, O living Lord!
Earth's bread and fruit you give in blessing;
    Forever be your name adored.

Psalm 67 is a classic psalm of praise, invoking God's blessing and calling on the entire nation to praise the Lord for his blessings among them. God judges with equity among all the nations. The language here recalls the Aaronic benediction (Num. 6:24–26) and may have been used as a priestly blessing of the people as they came to or left the temple at various agricultural festivals. Certainly, "The earth has yielded its increase; God, our God, has blessed us," would suggest as much. Interestingly, the Hebrew word for God's name, given to Moses at the burning bush, and rendered in English as "Lord," is missing here. Instead, the broader term for God, *Elohim*, is consistently used. Central to the psalm is the conviction that the God who has blessed "us" (Israel is never mentioned but assumed) is the God of all, and "all the ends of the earth" are called upon to revere, fear, and stand in awe before him.

Psalm 68

Verses 1–10, 32–35

CMD

ELLACOMBE

Rise up, O God, dispel your foes;
    Let all who hate you flee.
As smoke is vanquished by the wind,
    So let the wicked be.
But let the righteous sing for joy,
    Exulting in your fame.
You ride the winds in victory;
    The Lord God is your name.

The orphaned and the destitute
    Take refuge in your care.
And you become a dwelling place
    Where life is just and fair.
The homeless find their rest in you,
    And pris'ners find new life,
While all who work against your will
    Dwell in the midst of strife.

When you went out before us, Lord,
    To march across the land,
The earth quaked and the rains poured forth
    Before your mighty hand.
O God of Sinai, living Lord,
    You give new life, indeed,
Providing shelter, food, and hope
    For all who live in need.

Sing praise, O kingdoms of the earth;
    Before the Lord rejoice!
All hosts of heav'n, attune your ear
    To this almighty voice.

Majestic over Israel,
>The skies proclaim God's fame.
With awesome power God gives us strength;
>How blessed is God's name.

P salm 68 is a battle hymn remembering and celebrating the victories of the Lord on behalf of his people. It is complex in that it uses virtually all of the biblical names for God: *Elohim, El, Yah, Adonai, El Shaddai, Yah Elohim*, and *Yahweh*. It opens with the plea that those who hate the Lord will be driven out like smoke driven by the wind, as wax melts before a fire, that the wicked may perish. The righteous will be glad and rejoice in God and will sing to the Lord a new song. The prayer then turns to extolling God's justice and righteousness — a father to the orphan, an honest judge for the widow, a home for the lonely, one who leads prisoners to freedom. It is a mixture of high praise for the Lord, who dwells in his sanctuary among his people executing justice. It is also a description of various moments in Israel's life when the Lord has intervened to give them victory — from their release from captivity in Egypt, their travels through the wilderness, to their settling into the land of promise, and various wars and skirmishes thereafter. The land quaked at Sinai at the presence of the Lord. Rain clouds opened to give drink to his people. Kings fled before the Lord, giving the people peace and prosperity among the sheepfolds. The mountains of Bashan are celebrated (a place in the Transjordan, famous for raising cattle), but these mighty mountains envy Jerusalem, the mountain of God. The number of God's chariots is myriad — thousands upon thousands — and the Lord leads the people and is among them, while he imprisons those who have been taken captive. Ascribed to David, the psalm recalls a moment when the Lord has given the enemy into his hand. Verses 21 to 23 indulge in graphic battle language (evidently why those who developed the daily lectionary excluded it from the day's reading), but it reminds us of the brutality of war in any age. It then returns to blessing the Lord as a festival procession makes its way to the temple to celebrate God's presence in Jerusalem. Envoys come from far and wide to pay tribute. The kingdoms of the earth sing praises to the Lord, who rides above Israel with strength and victory. The psalm ends with one final ascription of praise: "the Lord gives strength and power to his people. Blessed be God!"

Psalm 69

Verses 6–16

8.7.8.7 D

BLAENHAFREN

Let my shame not touch your people,
    Lord; for you I bear this blame.
Like a stranger to my family,
    Sister, brother shun my name.
Still my zeal to know your presence
    Burns like fire, a growing flame.
Though I fast and dress in sackcloth,
    Still they ridicule my name.

As for me, yet will I serve you;
    Answer, Lord, when it is right.
Save me from the mud and insult;
    Hide me from my foes' delight.
Keep me from the rising water,
    Safe above the treach'rous sea.
Lord, remember your own promise;
    Steadfast mercy show to me.

Psalm 69 is the prayer of one who suffers and calls on the Lord for rescue from enemies and incorporates much of the vocabulary of biblical lament: "the floods sweep over me," "my eyes are weary with crying; my throat parched," "I am hated without cause," "have done no wrong," and so on. "Do not hide your face," "Answer me," "Do not let me be put to shame" are standard pleas in such laments. One unusual plea here is, "Do not let those who hope in you be put to shame because of me." The psalmist claims that this suffering, shame, abandonment by family and friends, and reproach are all being borne for God's sake. It is easy to see why writers of the New Testament so easily turned to this psalm as Old Testament prophecy of Jesus's life and passion, especially the portion of the psalm beyond today's appointed verses. As a result, this psalm took on new Messianic understanding, after the fact, for the way in which it seemed to prophetically foretell Jesus's innocent and vicarious suffering. However, the psalm takes a very human turn at verse 22, leaving the Messianic dimensions behind and turning imprecatory, invoking suffering upon enemies: "Pour out your indignation upon them," "May their camp be a desolation," "Add guilt to their guilt. . . . Let them be blotted out of the book of the living." The psalm then turns to a note of praise as it anticipates the Lord's faithful response to these pleas. Heaven and earth are called upon to join in praise as the psalm affirms that God will save Zion and rebuild Judah; and God's servants — those who love God's name — will live there in prosperity and peace.

Psalm 70

8.7.8.7 D

ENDLESS SONG, CONSTANCE

(*broken into four stanzas, the text can be sung to* DOMINUS REGIT ME)

Be pleased, O God, deliver me!
    O Lord, make haste to help me!
Confound all those who seek my life;
    Disgrace their lives completely.
Let those who seek to hurt my life
    Be heaped with great dishonor.
Let those who say, "Aha," "Aha,"
    Know shame instead of honor.

Let all who seek you, Lord, rejoice,
    Be glad, and know no sadness.
Let those who love your saving ways
    Say "God is great!" with gladness.
But I am poor and in great need;
    Make haste to my entreaty.
You are my help, my sole defense;
    O Lord, come to me quickly.

Psalm 70 is a short lament with petitions for help. It is one of the few laments in the Psalter that do not end with words of praise and triumph indicating that the Lord has already acted. The prayer opens on a word of urgency: "Make haste to help me!" The enemy is personal and is trying to bring shame and dishonor to the petitioner. Their taunts and jeers are described as "Aha, Aha!" It then pleads that all who seek God may be glad and rejoice and all who love and trust in God's salvation shall be able, evermore, to say, "God is great!" Confessing her need, she again pleads for God to "hurry up and help!" and then concludes with the confession that God is her help and her deliverer; and for the first time, God is named as "the Lord" and asked not to delay. This psalm, almost verbatim, is also found as the last five verses of Psalm 40.

Psalm 71

Verses 1–6
CM
SPOHR

To you, O Lord, I come for help,
     For refuge in your name.
In righteousness now hear my cry,
     And keep me safe from shame.

From wicked ones with cruel pow'rs,
     Lord, rescue me as proof
That you alone are hope and strength,
     My savior from my youth.

You are my hope, my trust, O Lord,
     Salvation in this hour.
On you, Lord, I have leaned from birth;
     You nurture me each hour.

Verses 7–14
7.7.7.7.7.7
REDHEAD NO. 76

Mocking crowds have scorned my name;
     Ridicule and hurt are mine.
Others point to my great shame,
     Making me a painful sign.
Lord, you are my strength and praise;
     I will trust you all my days.

Do not cast me off with age,
    Nor forsake me when I'm weak.
Enemies around me rage;
    My undoing still they seek.
Lord, you are my strength and praise;
    I will trust you all my days.

"Godforsaken one!" they cry.
    "None will come to offer aid."
O my God, prove that a lie,
    Quickly now, for they invade.
Lord, you are my strength and praise;
    I will trust you all my days.

O my God, stand not aloof
    As I call upon your name.
Be my enemies' reproof;
    Scorn all those who seek my shame.
Lord, you are my strength and praise;
    I will trust you all my days.

Psalm 71 is both a lament and a song of praise, and almost seems to be an extension of Psalm 70. If David did not write this, he should have! It is filled with the language of praise, trust, and assurance, and also with the continuing plea for God's sustaining and saving presence in the midst of the wicked who seek his life, as indeed, many sought David's life. But this is equally as important a prayer for us to pray through the seasons of our lives, as we continue to look to God to be for us a rock of refuge, a strong fortress that saves. From the moment of birth, when God began to watch over us, until our last breath, God will not forsake us but be our source of life and salvation. Therefore the psalmist shouts for joy and sings continuing praises to God.

Psalm 72

Verses 1–7, 10–14, 18–19

CMD

SALVATION

Give justice to your king, O Lord;
    Make righteousness his throne.
With fairness let him tend the poor,
    His upright ways your own.
May mountains yield prosperity,
    And hills your righteousness.
May he defend all those in need,
    And crush all wickedness.

As long as sun and moon endure,
    So make his days to be,
Like rain that falls on fresh-mown grass,
    Like show'rs on earth and sea.
In him may righteousness abound,
    And peace fill every land,
Until the moon shines forth no more;
    So bless us by his hand.

May kings from Tarshish and the isles
    Come forth and tribute bring;
The rulers of all other lands
    His sovereign praises sing.
He saves the needy when they call,
    Gives help to those who fear.
From violence he protects the poor;
    Their lives to him are dear.

Blest be the God of Israel,
    O Lord, how great your name.
Your wondrous ways are glorious;
    Your deeds are still the same.

Lord, may your glory fill the earth,
    In wondrous ways again.
Let every people bless your name
    And all things shout "Amen!"

Alternate version

LM

ST DROSTANE, DANBY, DICKINSON COLLEGE

Great God, whose universal way
    The known and unknown worlds obey,
Now give the kingdom to your Son,
    Your Holy and Anointed One.

Exalt your throne, extend your hand,
    'Til all submit to Christ's command.
His justice shall avenge the poor,
    And pride and rage shall be no more.

With power vindicate the just,
    And tread oppression into dust.
O, may Christ's reign and kingdom last,
    When hours and years and times are past.

As dawn spreads from the east to west,
    So shall Christ's name as King be blest.
As light brings healing in its rays,
    So may we serve Christ all our days.

The saints shall flourish in Christ's days,
    Arrayed in robes of joy and praise.
Peace like a river from God's throne
    Shall flow to worlds as yet unknown.

105

Adapted from 1843 *Psalms and Hymns* for the Psalter Task Force, PCUSA.

Psalm 72 is a royal psalm that prays for the king, the son of a king, and may have been used as King Solomon's annual enthronement liturgy. It extols the king's goodness, delivering the needy, having pity on the weak, saving the oppressed from violence, and holding them precious in his sight. The psalm intercedes for long life and all of its blessings, and that the king may continue to judge God's people with righteousness and justice. It ends by blessing the Lord as the God of Israel, who does wondrous things and stands behind the king's righteousness. May the Lord's name and glory fill the whole earth. "So be it; let it be!"

Psalm 77

Verses 1–2, 11–20
8.6.8.6.8.6
CAROL'S GIFT, MORNING SONG

Recall the wondrous works of God,
    The things the Lord has done.
Reflect on all God's mighty deeds;
    Give thanks for every one.
Cry out to God, who always hears,
    The Lord, the Holy One.

Your way, O God, is holiness;
    What god is great like you?
You are the God of wondrous deeds,
    Displayed for all to view.
Cry out to God, who always hears,
    The Lord, the Holy One.

With arms of strength you have redeemed
    The house of Israel.
The waters fled when you appeared,
    The fire and lightning fell.
Cry out to God, who always hears,
    The Lord, the Holy One.

The whirlwind lashed the sea and land;
    All at your presence shook.
You made a way straight through the sea,
    The path your people took.
Cry out to God, who always hears,
    The Lord, the Holy One.

You led your people like a flock,
    Joseph and Jacob's band.
Through Moses and through Aaron too,
    You took them by the hand.
Cry out to God, who always hears,
    The Lord, the Holy One.

Psalm 77 is a lament in time of trouble, asking, "Where is the Lord?" Will he remain absent forever? Through long, sleepless nights, the psalmist's soul is troubled. In that time of God's silence he occupies himself with remembering the mighty works of God who led Israel through the sea and to the land of promise. We can do no better in those times of our own trouble. Remembering God's work in our lives in a posture of thanksgiving has power to lift our spirits — thus the use of the theme, "Cry out to God, who always hears. . . ."

Psalm 78

Verses 1–4, 12–16

CMD

MAPLE AVENUE, HALIFAX; *may also be sung to* SOUTHERN SEMINARY

Give ear, my people, to my word,
   To teachings true and bold.
My mouth will speak in parables,
   Dark sayings from of old.
To children's children let us tell
   The triumphs for us won,
The glorious deeds we've known and heard,
   Of wonders God has done.

In Egypt, there the Lord did work
   Great marvels in the land.
The sea divided, making two,
   The deed of God's own hand.
The waters were blown back in heaps,
   Between them came dry land.
And thus our people were brought forth
   By God's almighty hand.

With clouds God led them in the day,
   With fiery light by night,
To guide them in the wilderness,
   To save them with great might.
The Lord split rocks to bring forth drink,
   To quench their deadly thirst,
Made streams gush forth from out of rocks
   When life seemed at its worst.

Give ear, my people, to my word,
 To teachings true and bold.
My mouth will speak in parables,
 Dark sayings from of old,
Things we have heard, and we have known,
 From ancient times foretold.
We will not hide these from our young
 But let God's truth unfold.

God gave decrees to Jacob's own,
 The law to Israel's kin,
Compelling us to teach our own,
 And keep them free from sin.
And so we speak of God's commands,
 Of statutes that we laud,
That generations yet unborn
 May set their hopes on God.

Psalm 78 is a psalm of praise for God's saving actions, but also recounts for a later generation their ancestors' continuing fickleness and faithlessness, in spite of God's gracious responses to their needs. The portion used here focuses on God's acts to redeem and save, and begins as a wisdom psalm, much of it built on two-strophe Hebrew parallelisms — the second line repeating, by way of synonym, what the first line has introduced. Though their ancestors witnessed God's power during the plagues in the fields of Zoan, in the Egyptian delta, and then in the division of the sea, the cloud by day and pillar of fire by night, and water coming forth from the rock, still, they were rebellious. "Can God spread a table in the wilderness?" they asked. But of course; that is precisely what God did. In spite of God's anger at their lack of faith in him, God continued to provide the things the psalm recounts in magnificent imagery — bread of angels, water gushing from the rock, birds falling at their feet around their camps. The psalmist thus recalls God's acts of provision during Israel's time in the wilderness.

Psalm 79

Verses 1–9
SMD
ICH HALTE TREULICH STILL, DIADEMATA

Your honor is defiled,
Your holy place undone.
The godless have swept o'er the land;
Jerusalem is doomed.
Deliver us, O God!
Take back your earthly throne.
In your compassion, save us Lord!
Reclaim us as your own.

Our people have been crushed,
And scattered 'cross the land,
Their bodies left to feed the birds,
Their blood dried in the sand.
How long, O Lord, how long?
Give up these wrath-filled days.
And for the glory of your name
Forgive our faithless ways.

Our neighbors' endless taunts
Deride us night and day.
Why should these godless ones succeed?
Pour out your wrath, we pray.
Come speedily to us,
And save us from their din.
Avenge your people's suffering;
Remember not our sin.

Why should the nations say,
"Where is their helpless God?"
Come demonstrate your pow'r to save

And raise us from the sod.
Salvation is your name;
For this you are well known.
Lord, for the glory of your name
Reclaim us as your own.

Psalm 79 is a communal lament that reveals the horror in and around Jerusalem when Babylon finally came and destroyed it in 587 BCE, burning the temple to the ground, slaughtering its people, and taking its leaders into exile. The psalmist pleads for God to give up his anger and jealous wrath at the people and stop all of the violence. Rather, pour forth that anger on the nations that have plundered Israel, those who do not know the Lord or call upon the Lord's name. The psalmist now offers an oblique confession of sin, pleading that God not remember against his people the sins of their ancestors, but, instead, respond speedily with compassion and help. The Lord is addressed as "the God of our salvation," and asked to act on Israel's behalf for the glory of his name. "Why should the nations say, 'Where is their God?'" Rather, give the nations what they have given us. Avenge us and let the nations know it is your vengeance, and let that be known among them before our eyes — vindicate us! Prayers are offered for God to preserve the prisoners carried off to Babylon who are doomed to die there. The psalmist then turns bitter and requests that those around them who taunted them and refused to come to their aid, while they watched Jerusalem under siege, receive sevenfold the taunts with which they taunted the Lord as Jerusalem fell. Notice that it is only after this complete retaliation is accomplished that the psalmist promises to give thanks to the Lord. "Then we your people, the flock of your pasture, will give thanks to you forever; from generation to generation we will recount your praise." The bitterness of the survivors of Jerusalem and their hatred of those around them who took advantage of their defeat is clearly resonant in this very human expression of grief and despair. Yet, it is a grief and despair that is still addressed to God. This is, of course, one of the glories of the Psalter: its ability to cast all of life, even its darkest moments of suffering and anguish, under the sovereignty and mercy of God.

Psalm 80

SM, *with refrain*
MARION, VINEYARD HAVEN *(preferred tune)*

O hear our cry, O Lord,
Now hear us as we pray.
You guide us as a shepherd leads,
So keep us in your way.
 O come, Lord, come,
 Restore and save us now.

Enthroned above all worlds,
You shine with holy light.
Lord, pour your pow'r upon us all,
And save us with your might.
 O come, Lord, come,
 Restore and save us now.

O Lord, the God of Hosts,
Turn not your face away.
Our tears have been both food and drink;
Foes mock us night and day.
 O come, Lord, come,
 Restore and save us now.

O Lord, our God, return;
Bring peace into each home.
So let your face shine on us all;
Restore us as your own.
 O come, Lord, come,
 Restore and save us now.

Psalm 80 is a community lament at the time of national disaster brought on by an oppressing superpower. Some scholars think it can be traced to 722 BCE when Assyria destroyed the northern kingdom — note the specific reference to Ephraim, Benjamin, and Manasseh, all northern tribes. It is directed to God as the "Shepherd of Israel," the one who leads Joseph's flock, enthroned in the heavens. "Restore us, O God; let your face shine, that we may be saved." This classic call for God's presence to rise up and destroy the enemy is repeated at the conclusion of each of the psalm's three sections. The first is an initial plea for salvation, the second, a description of Israel's troubles, and the third, a beautiful allegory of Israel as God's vine — uprooted from Egypt, brought into a new land and firmly planted there, but now in jeopardy of full destruction. "How long will you be angry with your people's prayers?" — their worship. From this psalm come the memorable phrases "bread of tears" and "tears to drink in full measure." Near the end, it prays for God's presence and strength for the king, the one at God's right hand whom God has made strong for God's purposes. Later, this phrase will take on Messianic tones. For the psalmist, it is a plea for God to rise up and restore his people.

Psalm 81

Verses 1, 10–16

CMD

ALL SAINTS NEW, MINERVA, KINGSFOLD

Sing out with joy to God our strength,
    The God of Jacob praise,
Who brought us forth from Egypt's grip,
    From slav'ry did us save;
Who promised to provide for us,
    To nurture and to feed,
To fill our mouths with all good things,
    To give us all we need.

But we your people would not hear,
    Nor listen to your voice.
Our selfish wills would not submit,
    Nor make your way our choice.
You gave us to our stubborn hearts,
    Their counsel to obey;
We turned from all your promises,
    To walk in our own way.

You plead for us to hear your voice,
    To hearken and obey.
You promise to subdue our foes,
    And sweep them all away.
You pledge to give us all we need,
    With finest wheat supply,
And give us honey from the rock,
    Rich food to satisfy.

P salm 81 calls the people to a liturgical assembly on a festival day. They are to sing, shout for joy, raise a song, sound the musical instruments,

115

and blow the shofar (ram's horn) at the new moon (perhaps the feast of Passover, Pentecost, or Tabernacles). The reference to Joseph may mean this was composed in the Northern Kingdom during a Levite reform. The psalm turns prophetic and introduces the voice of God, remembering that he has relieved their shoulder of the burden of Egypt. They called and God answered. God tested them at the waters of Meribah (Exodus 17). Now, they are to listen, as God admonishes them. If only they would listen! There are to be no strange gods among them, nor are they to bow down to them. This is the Lord speaking, who brought them out of Egypt. If they would but open wide their mouths, the Lord would fill them. But the people did not listen and would not submit. And so God gave them over to their stubborn hearts. Once again the Lord extends the plea: If only they would listen and walk in God's ways. Then God would quickly subject their enemies; turn his hand against their foes, causing those who hate him to cringe. For their own part, God would feed them with the finest of wheat and honey from the rock. It initially seems quite remarkable how often these themes need to appear, causing one to wonder why the people did not respond. But then, the Israelites were making a transition from being a nomadic, pastoral people to those who depended upon agriculture, and Baalism was a fertility religion that focused on Baal ensuring the crops. Notice how often the Lord promises to fill them with good things if they but turn to him. Now, think of how easily you and I are drawn away from trusting the Lord when other, more tangible and more practical solutions seem to be at hand.

Psalm 82

CMD

KINGSFOLD

Within the courts of the divine,
    Where holy judgment lives,
God sits among the sons of God,
    And heaven's judgment gives.
How long will you corruptly judge,
    O rulers of the earth?
How long will you love wickedness
    And cultivate its curse?

Give justice to the weak and lost,
    The orphan and bereft.
Maintain the right of all the weak,
    The lowly and distressed.
Deliver them from wicked hands,
    From those who plot for gain.
Uphold their rights within the land,
    And seek to ease their pain.

You sovereigns of the nations hear:
    Your judgments are unfair.
You rule in darkened ignorance;
    The earth shakes in despair.
I made you gods, my own offspring,
    Children of the Most High,
Yet like all mortals you shall fall,
    Like every prince shall die.

The earth cries out in its despair;
　Its peoples plead "How long?"
They pray for justice and for peace,
　A world where all belong.
Rise up, O God, and judge the earth;
　The nations are your own.
Give justice to this world you love;
　Come, make your ways our own.

Psalm 82 sounds less like a hymn than it does an oracle of judgment against the rulers of the earth. God has assembled the leaders of the peoples and is holding court in the midst of "the gods," not the gods of the foreign nations, but the angelic beings that form the heavenly court and are the Lord's servants. He passes judgment on the rulers of the peoples: How long will they judge unjustly and show partiality to the wicked? They are appointed to give justice to the weak and the orphan and to maintain the right of the lowly and the destitute. All rulers in the Bible are regularly reminded that the measure of their faithfulness is how they care for the poor and the destitute, something it would be well for our elected officials to remember. They are accountable to one sovereign over both their electorate and their constitution! But, the problem is not new: the rulers assembled before God do not get it; they do not understand, walking around in darkness so that the foundations of earth are shaken. God then addresses them again: "You are gods, children of the Most High, all of you." It is a startling statement in scripture. They have been appointed to govern on God's behalf and failed. Though thought of as gods by their people, they shall die like every mortal, and fall like any prince. And now the psalm turns to prayer as the psalmist calls on God to rise up and judge the earth and bring the justice God desires in all places, for all the nations of the earth belong to God. The universal theology behind Second Isaiah is clearly woven deeply into this psalm.

Psalm 84

7.6.7.6 D

MERLE'S TUNE, AURELIA, EIGHTH DAY *(© Donald L. Clapper)*

How lovely is your dwelling,
O Lord, the God of Hosts.
We hunger for your presence;
In you alone we boast.
Our hearts long for your courtyard,
To dwell there all our days.
How blest are those who trust you,
And live to sing your praise.

The sparrow and the swallow
Find safety there and rest.
Within your shelt'ring presence,
They build their young a nest.
We place our lives before you,
Just as they place their own.
Like them we seek your presence,
To make your courts our home.

How blest are those who seek you,
And find your pathway true.
Their hearts walk down your highway;
They find their strength in you.
When passing through deep sorrow,
Springs well up from their tears,
To clothe the land with blessings,
To strengthen all their years.

O Lord of Hosts, our refuge,
Look now upon our need.
A day within your presence
Outshines all else, indeed.
To lie beyond your threshold,
To call upon your name,
Exceeds life lived in riches,
In luxury and fame.

How lovely is your dwelling,
O Lord and God of all.
We hunger for your presence;
Upon your name we call!
We place our lives before you,
As off'rings filled with praise.
How blest are those who trust you,
And serve you all their days.

Psalm 84 is a reflection on the wonders and gifts of abiding in God's dwelling place, and one of the most beautiful psalms in the entire collection. The well-known psalm, set so masterfully by Johannes Brahms in his German requiem on the occasion of his mother's death, celebrates the beauty of the temple as God's dwelling place among the people, as well as the psalmist's longing and desire to be there in God's presence. In the temple all are cared for — even the lowly sparrow and swallow are welcome at God's altar. It is worth the dangerous and difficult journey as they go from "strength to strength" on their pilgrimage to Zion and its temple, for a day there in its courts is better than a thousand elsewhere. Better a life of modest service at God's threshold, than a life of luxury and ease among the wicked. For the Lord is light and protection, the source of all good for those who walk in God's ways, and the source of happiness for all who trust in him.

Psalm 85

10.10.10.10.10

SONG 1, FINLANDIA

Lord God, you once showed favor to your land;
    Jacob's own fortunes once you did restore.
The people's own iniquity forgiv'n,
    You pardoned all their sin, and so much more.
In gracious love you turned away your wrath;
    Your anger hot against them did not last.

O saving God, restore us once again;
    Your indignation t'ward us put aside.
Will your hot anger not be turned away?
    Will our own children's children thus abide?
In steadfast love revive us, hear our voice!
    That we in your salvation may rejoice.

Let me now hear what you, Lord God, will say.
    Speak peace to us, your people, your own band.
Unto the faithful whose own hearts return,
    Your pow'r to save is constantly at hand
To those who trust your ways and in them stand;
    That your own glory may dwell in our land.

Your steadfast love and faithfulness will meet;
    True righteousness and peace will then embrace.
Then from the ground your faithfulness will spring,
    And righteousness shine forth from your own face.
So to our land, Lord, give a good increase,
    And righteousness now pave our steps in peace.

P salm 85 is a communal lament of petition that is preceded by reminding God of how he has been favorable to the people in the past, restoring the fortunes of Jacob, forgiving the people's iniquity and pardoning all their sin, withdrawing his wrath and turning from his hot anger. And so the plea is now, "Restore us again." "Will you be angry forever?" "Revive us again so that your people may rejoice in you. Show us your steadfast love, O Lord, and grant us your salvation." Whether the psalmist himself or a priest in the temple, one now speaks prophetically and says, "Let me hear what God the Lord will speak," and then promises, "God will speak peace to his people, to his faithful ones, to those who turn to him in their hearts." For these, salvation is at hand. The result of this is that steadfast love and faithfulness will meet; righteousness and peace will kiss; faithfulness will spring up from the ground and righteousness will look down from the sky. As a sign of God's favor, these four cardinal and classic attributes of God will be upon those who turn to him. The land will yield its increase, and righteousness will go before the Lord, making a path for their steps.

Psalm 86

Verses 1–10, 16–17

CMD

MAPLE AVENUE, GRATUS, SEACHRIST

Incline your ear, Lord, answer me;
    I'm poor and filled with need.
Preserve my life and loyalty;
    Unto my trust give heed.
You are my God, all day I call:
    Be gracious, Lord, be true.
Come gladden now your servant's soul;
    I lift it up to you.

For you, O Lord, are good and kind,
    Forgiving in your ways.
Your steadfast love abounds for all
    Who seek you all their days.
Give ear, O Lord, unto my prayer;
    Now listen to my cry.
In troubled days I call on you,
    And wait for your reply.

There is no other like you, Lord,
    None worthy of our praise.
The nations you have made shall come
    To bless you all their days.
For you are great; your works astound,
    Each worthy of our laud.
Your deeds are wondrous, like your ways,
    For you alone are God!

Now turn to me in graciousness;
    Lord, listen to my plea.

Your servant favor with a sign
   To shame my enemy.
Show them and all who hate my life
   That you are God, indeed,
For you have been my help and strength,
   My comfort in all need.

Psalm 86 is an individual's plea for God's help that is classic in its structure and content. It begins calling on God to listen, knowing that it is God's disposition to hear and to answer. The psalmist is "poor and needy," for whatever reason, as yet, we do not know. The plea to preserve his life is coupled with a reminder of his devotion to God, followed by the same plea in a different form: save your servant who trusts in you. The plea continues, always issued out of a confession of God's character: gracious, good, forgiving, and abounding in steadfast love for all who call upon him — as the psalmist is now calling. After the initial plea, the psalmist sings a hymn of praise that echoes the themes we also hear in Second Isaiah. The Lord alone is God; there is no other like him. He has made everything, including the nations, and all are his. They shall all come and bow before the Lord and give glory to God's name. Now there comes another petition, this less focused on a pressing danger, and more a general plea for the gift of faithfulness: "Teach me your way, O Lord, that I may walk in your truth; give me an undivided heart . . . ," a marvelous phrase expressing the desire to have the capacity to live in total orientation to God and God's ways. Confessing again the greatness of the Lord as well as God's steadfast love — that he has already delivered him from the depths of Sheol — he now comes to the point of present need: a band of insolent ruffians has risen against him and seeks his life, a people who do not serve or observe God's ways. The Lord's mercy, grace, resistance to anger, and steadfast love and faithfulness are all affirmed as a context for seeking it now, as expressed in a classic Hebrew parallelism: "Give strength to your servant; save the child of your serving girl." It is a request not only for help, but so that those who hate him may see it and be put to shame, because they have seen the Lord helping and comforting him. As always, the act of prayer draws the petitioner into a relationship with God that, in and of itself, provides much of what is being sought — an experience of help and comfort.

Psalm 89

Verses 1–4, 19–26
11.10.11.10
CHARTERHOUSE, VICAR

Your steadfast love, O Lord, I'll sing forever;
To all I will declare your faithfulness.
Your love and mercy proven true forever,
As firm as heaven is your steadfastness.

You said to David, "You are my own chosen;
This covenant I now swear unto you:
I will establish you and yours forever,
And build your throne forever, sound and true."

You spoke in vision to your faithful prophets,
"Upon a mighty one I give my pow'r.
With holy oil I have anointed David;
With strength my hand shall bear him every hour.

"The wicked shall not bring him to submission,
Nor enemies outwit him in his ways.
His foes I'll crush, destroy all those who hate him;
My steadfast love will keep him all his days.

"In my own name his strength shall be exalted;
His realm from sea to rivers shall extend.
He shall cry out, 'O Lord, you are my Father,
My God, my faithful Rock, unto the end!'"

"With holy oil I have anointed David;
My hand and strength remain with him always.
The wicked shall not bring him to submission,
Nor enemies outwit him all his days.

"His foes I'll crush; I'll strike all those who hate him,
My steadfast love will keep him to the end.
In my own name his strength shall be exalted,
His realm from sea to rivers shall extend.

"He shall cry out, 'O Lord, you are my Father,
My God, my saving Rock, my very own!'
The firstborn and the highest king I'll make him,
Of every king on earth who mounts a throne.

"Forever in my steadfast love I'll keep him,
My covenant with him forever sure.
His line I will establish strong forever,
His throne as long as heaven shall endure.

"If his descendants flee from my instruction,
If they forsake my laws, fall into sin,
Then I will punish them for their transgressions,
But not remove my faithful love from him.

"My covenant I will not break or alter;
My words of promise I will never shun.
By my own holiness I've sworn to David;
His throne shall live before me like the sun."

Psalm 89 celebrates not only God's sovereignty over all, it remembers God's covenant with David and prays that God will continue to preserve and protect David and his reign forever and reestablish David's royal line. In all probability, this psalm was written while Israel was in exile in Babylon (587–538 BCE). The psalm remembers God's faithfulness to David and speaks of the unique relationship that God and David have with one another. It recounts God's promise to David, not only that he is the Lord's anointed, but that one of his sons will reign forever, "as long as the heavens endure." David calls out to God as "My father," and God makes him the firstborn, "the highest of the kings of the earth." God will forever keep his steadfast love for David and the covenant with him. But if David's children forsake God's law, do not walk after its ordinances, violate its statutes, and do not keep God's commandments, then God will punish their transgressions. Nonetheless, God will not remove or violate this covenant, nor take his steadfast love from David. Once and for all God has sworn by his holiness: "I will not lie to David. His line will continue forever," shining before God like the sun.

Psalm 90

LM

PENTECOST, ANGELUS, ROCKINGHAM OLD, GOD AND KING

Lord, you have been our dwelling place,
A refuge where our feet have trod.
Before you placed all things in space,
From everlasting you are God.

Your words can turn us back to dust;
Our lives are fragile like a dream.
As grass that sprouts yet fades at dusk,
We're born, we live, but pass unseen.

Our years are but three score and ten;
With special health they reach four score.
But still they're filled with pain and sin,
Soon gone and then we live no more.

So teach us how to count our days,
That wisdom might fill all our time.
Return, O Lord, accept our praise,
That through our lives your love may shine.

Establish, Lord, the work we do,
And through it make your glory known,
That praise may ever come to you,
And unto all, your love be shown.

Psalm 90 reflects on the majesty and awesomeness of God and the frailty and limitedness of human beings, as it ponders life's meaning. Whereas God has existed from everlasting to everlasting and for him a thousand years is but a moment, our days are short, like grass that sprouts in the morning, flourishes midday, and by evening fades and withers. Our days pass away under God's wrath. Wrath here is both a symbol of God's anger or disapproval at the ways of humanity, and also a symbol of God's constant plea for humanity to return to the purposes for which we were first brought into being. Our days are lived out under that watchful eye and then come to an end, like a sigh. They are seventy, perhaps eighty years with good health, but still, they are filled with toil and trouble, and too soon gone. Given all this, the psalmist asks for wisdom to count our days, and therein to gain some wisdom. Finally, the Lord is called on by name and asked to turn from wrath to compassion. "Satisfy us in the morning with your steadfast love so that we may rejoice and be glad all our days." God is asked to make us as glad as the many days God has afflicted us. More: let God's work be manifest in our own work, thereby giving it meaning and purpose. The concluding benediction is bold in its request that life be good and meaningful: "Let the favor of the Lord our God be upon us." The psalm concludes with this final, direct, and bold request: "Prosper for us the work of our hands — O prosper the work of our hands!"

Psalm 91

8.7.8.7 D
ABBOTT'S LEIGH

Dwelling in your shelter, O Lord,
    Living in your strength and shade,
Here's a place of trustful accord,
    And a fortress for our aid.
You with sure defense protect us,
    And your judgments are all just.
Safe from hidden dangers keep us!
    Living Lord, in you we trust.

Shaded by your sheltering wings,
    We find safety in your care:
Sure defense and faithful refuge,
    Rescue from life's pain and snare.
Thus we shall not fear night's terror,
    Nor the arrow in the day,
Plague nor sickness, human error;
    Lord, you are life's strength and stay.

Those who make you their defender
    Find protection in your way.
There's no violence that can render
    Hurt, disaster, or decay.
For your mighty angels guard us,
    Bringing safety as they go.
With your strength their hands protect us,
    That life's hurts we may not know.

Lord, you save all those who love you,
    All who know you as their Lord.
When in fear we call upon you,

Rescue comes as your reward.
You endow us with salvation,
    And you take away our strife.
Trust in you brings celebration,
    For you give eternal life.

Alternate version
CM
ST. PETER, ST. ANNE

All those who dwell in God's cool shade,
    Cast by the Rock most high,
Sing "Lord, My refuge and my Rock,
    On you I will rely."

There is no terror morn or night,
    No weapon in the day,
Nor crisis rising like the sun,
    To burn our life away.

A thousand may beside us fall,
    Ten thousand at our hand;
Destruction will not come to us,
    For Lord, in you we stand.

Because we call the Lord our God,
    No evil shall befall.
Our lives, our homes, our every breath;
    God watches over all.

The angels have been giv'n to us
    To watch o'er all our ways;
Upon their wings they bear us still
    And will through all our days.

Because we hold to you in love,
   You hold us stronger still.
You shower us with life and strength;
   Salvation is your will.

Psalm 91, a song of trust and confidence, is one of the most assuring in the entire collection of 150 psalms. Though it reflects the theology of the wisdom tradition, insisting that those who remain righteous shall have the constant protection of the Lord, it is even richer in its imagery and promises. The opening line, "He who (which can also be translated 'You who,' or 'Those who') lives in the shelter of the Most High (*Elyon* — an ancient name for God), who abides in the shadow of the Almighty (*El Shaddai* — a second name for God), will say to the Lord (*Yahweh* — God's personal name given to Moses at the bush), 'My refuge, my fortress, my God in whom I trust.'" All three names are included to make this as comprehensive as possible, with the primacy given to the name *Yahweh*. Various forms of protection are mentioned, including the presence of God's angels to defend us in times of warfare or pestilence, and all other forms of danger. Under God's wings we will find a refuge, whose faithfulness is a buckler and a shield, so that we need not fear anything night or day. Making the Lord our refuge assures protection. It is from this psalm that Satan quotes as he tempts and challenges Jesus to throw himself off the tower of the temple, trusting that God will save him. The psalm concludes with God's own speech: "You who love me I will deliver. You who know my name I will protect. When you call (the importance of knowing God's name, knowing whom to call upon), I will answer; when in trouble, I will rescue and honor you. With long life I will satisfy you and show you my salvation." Is it any wonder this has been the byword and hope of Jews, Christians, and Muslims? This psalm is a favorite of military chaplains, frequently read before a group of soldiers facing battle. It is also regularly read at funerals and memorial services and times of grave national distress.

Psalm 92

8.7.8.7 D

OMNI DIE, WEISSE FLAGGEN

It is good to give you thanks, Lord,
    And to sing your praise, Most High,
To declare your love each morning,
    And at night, on you rely.
With the sound of lute and lyre,
    And the harp's rich melody,
I will praise your works with gladness,
    For the joy they give to me.

Great, indeed, are all your doings;
    Lord, your thoughts are very deep!
Though the dullard cannot know them,
    Nor the stupid ever keep.
Though the wicked sprout and flourish,
    And their evil works prevail,
You have doomed them to destruction;
    All your enemies will fail.

But my strength you have exalted,
    Like an ox within the wild.
You have poured fresh oil upon me,
    Marking me as your dear child.
My assailants' doom is certain;
    Their sure downfall do I see.
And my ears hear of their failure,
    As from them you set me free.

Yet, the righteous ones shall flourish,
    Like the palms and cedars grand.
Planted in your house and courtyards,

In your presence they shall stand.
Though they age, their fruit is endless;
They are green and full of life.
Thus they show you always upright,
Faithful, true in every strife.

Psalm 92 is a hymn of thanksgiving, and identified in its header as a song for the sabbath. It is perfectly suited for remembering and praising the Lord in sabbath rest, when the worshiper is to reflect on God's goodness. The hours of prayer are cited, as well as the music to accompany such prayer in the temple. The Lord has made the psalmist glad by God's work. At the sight of it, the psalmist sings for joy. He then turns to reflect upon what God has done. The dullard cannot know and the stupid cannot understand the ways of God. Though the wicked sprout like grass, they are doomed to destruction forever, for the Lord will destroy his enemies. In addition, the Lord has exalted the psalmist's strength (horn), like that of a wild ox, and poured fresh oil upon him in blessing. His eyes have seen the downfall of his personal enemies and his ears have heard of the doom of his assailants. The psalm ends in typical wisdom tradition, with the affirmation that the righteous will flourish like the palm tree and grow like the cedar of Lebanon planted in courts of the house of the Lord. In old age, they continue to be fruitful, full of strength and sexual potency — showing that the Lord is upright and a rock to those who fear him. "There is no unrighteousness in him."

Psalm 93

CMD

VOX DILECTI, MINERVA

The Lord our God rules over all,
    None can escape this reign.
All nations, peoples, pow'rs on earth
    Shall bow before God's name.
With majesty our Lord is clothed,
    All things are in God's care.
There is no pow'r nor earthly force
    That can with God compare.

Flood, earthquake, pestilence, and war
    Still threaten life on earth.
Yet those whose confidence is God
    Are given strength and worth.
Our God almighty dwells on high,
    This care is daily proved.
From Adam to the final day,
    God's world shall not be moved.

All hope is sure for those who live
    Life centered in God's word.
No earthly leader, pow'r, or might
    Can keep us more assured.
The Lord our God rules over all,
    And promises the same,
Life, blessing, hope, and confidence,
    To all who trust God's name.

Psalm 93, probably used during the annual enthronement of Israel's king, has been appropriated by the church for Easter because in his resurrection, Jesus has become King of kings and Lord of lords. The psalmist praises the majesty, strength, and holiness of the Lord — Israel's true king — and recalls how all creation has been established by God and shall not be moved. So too is God's throne firmly fixed from of old and is "until everlasting." Even the floods join their voices in praising God's majesty. God's reign is eternal, God's decrees are sure, and only holiness is suitable for God's house. In the enthronement, this psalm reminds Israel's king of who it is who truly reigns in Israel, and to whom he is accountable — the Lord.

Psalm 94

7.6.7.6 D

LLANGLOFFAN

O Lord, the God of vengeance,
  Come forth and judge the earth.
Bring havoc on the wicked;
  Give righteousness its worth.
The evil seem to prosper;
  Will them you not assail?
Come, Lord, avenge your people;
  Let righteousness prevail.

The wicked crush your people
  With deadly word and deed.
The orphan and the widow
  Are victims of their greed.
They say, "God does not see us.
  The Lord does not perceive!"
And so they slay the stranger,
  While none among them grieve.

Such arrogance is deadly;
  When, fools, will you be wise?
The Source of sight and hearing
  Can see and hear your lies.
The Lord knows what you're thinking;
  God sees through your deceit.
The One who judges nations
  Will see to your defeat.

Psalm 94 asks, "Fools, when will you be wise? Do you not remember that the Lord rises up against the arrogant?" The One who made the ear and the eye, do you think he does not hear or see? The Lord stands against the wicked, and disciplines and chastises nations so that justice may return to the widow, the orphan, and the outsider. In the midst of those who oppress, the psalmist gives thanks that the Lord is his avenger, stronghold, rock, and refuge, whose consolations cheer the downcast soul.

Psalm 95

8.7.8.7.7.7

UNSER HERRSCHER

Come and sing to God our Savior.
 Let us make a joyful noise,
For the Lord is our salvation,
 And the source of all our joys.
Lord, we come into this place
 Singing songs of love and grace.

You are mighty, great, and glorious,
 Sovereign over all that is.
All the worlds are your possession,
 Earth and sky and all that lives.
All are firmly in your hand,
 Peoples, planets, sea, and land.

Worship, honor, love we bring you,
 Prayers of thanks and hymns of praise.
You have named us your possession,
 You, our guide for all our days.
Shepherd God whose ways are true,
 Hear us as we worship you.

Listen to God's supplication:
 "Harden not your hearts again,
As you tested me at Massah,
 Putting me to proof therein.
Those who like them go astray,
 Shall not know my rest or stay."

Psalm 95 begins calling the congregation to worship, singing for joy to the Lord, who is the rock of our salvation, calling worshipers to come before him with joyful psalms (rather than bulls, goats, or other sacrificial animals). This may indicate that the psalm was not composed until after the loss of the temple in 587 BCE and the Babylonian exile, when the rabbis began to define prayer and praise as another form of sacrifice to the Lord. The Lord is described as "a great God, and a great King above all gods," indicating that though Israel might now be monotheistic in its worship, it still considered there to be other gods over which the Lord is sovereign, rather than the Lord being the only god. Rather, he is the God of gods. Consequently, the Lord's sovereignty over all creation is described in traditional ways: depths of the earth, heights of the mountains, seas, dry land, and so on. Though God is sovereign over all, God is also Maker and Shepherd of the people, who are here called to "bow down" before and listen to, rather than test their Maker. Then the Lord speaks, warning, "Do not harden your hearts," as the people did at Meribah and Massah, moments in the exodus wilderness wandering (Exod. 17:1–7) that led to God's judgment that they would not enter God's rest. It is a reference to their forty years of wandering and God's loathing of them, and the consequent loss of the rest that could have come to them by entering the land of promise immediately, as well as to the sabbath rest that is emblematic of sharing in God's abiding presence.

Psalm 96

LM, *with Alleluias*
LASST UNS ERFREUEN

O sing to God a joyful song;
Come all on earth and join the throng.
Blest are you, Lord, our Creator;
You bring salvation day by day,
Both in our work and in our play.
Blest are you, Lord, our Creator,
Alleluia, Alleluia, Alleluia.

Lord, all the nations praise your pow'r;
They stand assembled in this hour.
Great are you, Lord, King of nations;
Truth, power, majesty, and fame,
Beauty and glory form your name.
Great are you, Lord, King of nations,
Alleluia, Alleluia, Alleluia.

All you who gather here to pray,
Lift up your hearts and with us say:
"Blest are you, Lord, our Redeemer."
Here in this court with love comply,
Offer your life, on God rely.
Bless the Lord, our great Redeemer,
Alleluia, Alleluia, Alleluia.

Let all creation burst in song,
Sea, field, and forest, teeming throng —
We exalt you, living Savior.
Come, Holy Lord, and judge the earth;
O come in judgment, bring new birth.
We exalt you, living Savior,
Alleluia, Alleluia, Alleluia.

P salm 96 celebrates God's goodness as King, and calls on all creation to "sing a new song to the Lord!" It celebrates the goodness of God's sovereignty over all things and is a reminder that God is not only sovereign, but judge, and will judge with righteousness and truth. Every line is a call to worship. It is, perhaps, the finest example of a hymn of praise we have in the entire Psalter, filled with familiar and beautiful words and phrases that praise and thank God. In addition, it keeps before us the important truth that God not only reigns in goodness, but is coming in judgment that is righteousness and truth — another form of God's goodness — and justice will ultimately be done.

Psalm 97

8.7.8.7.8.7

IRBY, HOLYWOOD, WESTMINSTER ABBEY *(preferred tune)*

Lord, you reign, the earth rejoices;
    All the coastlands shout with glee.
Clouds mysterious form around you;
    Justice is your constant plea.
Fire goes forth consuming evil;
    Justice is your constant plea.

All the heav'ns proclaim your goodness;
    Mountains melt before your face.
Lightning flashes bring your brightness,
    Giving light to every place.
You are Lord and King forever,
    Giving light to every place.

All the heav'ns proclaim your power;
    All the people praise your name.
Those who worship empty idols,
    Boasting still, are put to shame.
Righteous are your judgments ever;
    Those who boast are put to shame.

We who love you, Lord, hate evil;
    You respond to our complaints.
From the hand of wicked plotters,
    You protect the lives of saints.
You bring light into our darkness;
    You protect the lives of saints.

143

To our God, Divine Creator,
  To our Christ the Living Son.
To the Spirit, God's own presence,
  Ever three yet ever one,
Holy One, to you forever,
  Let all thanks and praise be sung.

P salm 97 celebrates God's sovereign rule over all the earth — not just
Israel! — and utilizes material from other psalms as well as many
themes from Second Isaiah (40–55), creating a hymn of praise that recognizes the Lord as not only Israel's King, but sovereign over all creation.
References to lightning and storm challenge the notion that those were
the works of the Canaanite god Baal. Not simply the earth, but the heavens as well, proclaim God's glory. Though nothing can fully contain God's
glory, the psalm puts to shame those who bow down before worthless
idols. For the Lord is not simply a god, but God of all the gods. This is a
conviction that emerged in Israel upon its return from Babylon. The Lord
had rescued them from the land of the wicked and now continues to "sow
light for the righteous," leading them in God's way. "Rejoice then in the
Lord, O you righteous. Give thanks to God's holy name!"

Psalm 98

8.7.8.7 D

AUSTRIAN HYMN, IN BABILONE

Sing a new song to our Savior
    For the marvels God has done.
Lord, your hand has brought us triumph,
    And revealed your vict'ry won.
Steadfast love and constant caring
    To your people you have shown.
All the earth has seen your glory
    And your goodness to your own.

Make a joyful noise, all people;
    Earth break forth in joyful song.
Organ, trumpet, bells, and cymbals
    Come and join the singing throng.
For our God is your own Maker,
    Saving all who turn in need.
Lift your hearts to sing new praises,
    For our God is King indeed.

Let the sea and all that fills it
    Roar with praise like crashing waves.
Let the waters shout in cascade
    For the Savior of our days.
Hills break forth to sing with laughter
    At the coming of our King.
Right and holy are the judgments
    Which our sovereign God shall bring.

Psalm 98 exhorts us to "Sing to the Lord a new song!" But the imperative is about more than us; all creation is called on to sing joyfully for what the Lord has done — marvelous things! Israel is called to remember the way the Lord has gotten victory for them in the midst of the nations. In their distress, the Lord remembered his steadfast love for them and his faithfulness to them, and vindicated them in the sight of their captors. All the ends of the earth have seen God's victory on Israel's behalf. The earth is especially called to join in the song of praise using all the musical instruments at hand: lyre, lute, trumpets, and horns. The personification of aspects of creation is rich and expressive: let the sea roar, and all who live in it; let the floods clap their hands and the hills together break into song at the presence of the Lord, for he is coming to judge the earth. And when he comes, he will judge the entire world with righteousness, and its peoples with equity. Joy to the world! Isaac Watts paraphrased this psalm into that well-known and deeply loved hymn. Though most think it was written as a Christmas carol, it is really a metrical setting of this psalm.

Psalm 99

LMD

JERUSALEM

Lord, you are King; we stand in awe
    To see you seated there on high.
You sit above the cherubim,
    And earth shakes with its own reply.
In Zion you are Lord and King,
    Exalted still, and long adored.
Let every people praise your name,
    Proclaiming, "You are holy, Lord."

O Sovereign One, you love the right;
    You work for justice constantly.
Among your people you have brought
    A fair and righteous equity.
Praise to you, Lord, for justice done;
    You, Lord, are God, the only one.
We come in praise before your throne,
    Proclaiming, "You are holy, Lord!"

Moses and Aaron were your priests,
    And Samuel called upon your name.
They cried to you in their own need;
    You answered them in cloud and flame.
You spoke your word from pillared cloud:
    Commands and statutes and decrees.
And they obeyed the words you spoke,
    For you are holy, living Lord.

147

O Lord, our God, you answered them;
    You were forgiving of their wrong.
But still you called them to account
    For all the sins that they had done.
We come to sing your praise, O Lord,
    And worship at your holy hill.
We will exalt your name in song,
    Proclaiming, "You are holy, Lord!"

Alternate version
8.8.8.8
O FILI ET FILIAE

You, Lord, are King, the people quake;
You sit enthroned, the mountains shake,
Exalted for your own name's sake.
Praise to your name, O Holy One.

From old, our people called on you,
Our prophets, priests, our leaders too.
You answered with your statutes true.
Praise to your name, O Holy One.

A mighty King, you love the right,
Creating justice day and night.
Come worship and proclaim God's might.
Praise to your name, O Holy One.

O Lord, our God, you answer still,
Forgiving, yet you do your will.
Come worship at God's holy hill.
Praise to your name, O Holy One.

P salm 99 is a psalm of praise that extols the Lord's holiness and sovereign power — the mighty King of the universe — who is also a lover of justice. The Lord is enthroned on the cherubim in the Holy of Holies in the temple; let the whole earth quake. For God is not only sovereign in power, but has also established equity, justice, and righteousness among Jacob's people. This, the last of the psalms that praise God as King, was and continues to be used in the church as a celebration of Jesus's resurrection, ascension, and triumphant reign. Because the church of the New Testament regarded the psalms as the work of the prophet David, it quickly understood him to be writing about his greater son, the Messiah. As Moses, Aaron, and Samuel all went before the Lord on Israel's behalf, so also did Christ go into heaven on our behalf. This psalm then blesses God for being forgiving, but also remembers God's need to avenge wrongdoing. The psalm ends calling on everyone to extol, praise, and worship the Lord at his holy mountain.   149

Psalm 100

LM

PUER NOBIS NASCITUR

Sing to the Lord, all worlds that are;
Sing songs of joy both near and far.
Come worship God with each new day;
With joyful hearts come sing and pray.

Our Lord is God, let none forget;
God made us all, God claims us yet.
Our Lord is shepherd, guide, and stay,
Protecting us in every way.

So enter here with joyful heart;
Lift up your voice, come take your part.
Come bless the Lord's own steadfast ways;
God's love shall last beyond our days.

Psalm 100 is one of the best known in the Psalter, primarily because of its role in metrical psalmody, though I suspect most think it a hymn rather than a psalm. "All people that on earth do dwell, sing to the Lord with cheerful voice. Him serve with mirth, his praise forth tell; come ye before him and rejoice." With these words, William Kethe paraphrased this classic psalm of praise and thanksgiving in 1560. The worshiper is called to the temple to sing God's praise as her maker, and to recognize that she lives among a people who are not only the sheep of God's hand but God's treasured flock. The Hebrew text has an important alternate version of this: "It is he that made us, and not we ourselves." Tradition in translation has gone with the previous reading because it was favored by the rabbis. "Enter his gates with thanksgiving" is followed by the parallel, "and his courts with praise." The final affirmation is a summary of all 150 psalms: "For the Lord is good; his steadfast love endures forever, and his faithfulness to all generations."

Psalm 103

Verses 1–14, 22
8.7.8.7 D
HYFRYDOL

Bless the Lord with all my being;
    All within me bless God's name.
Bless the Lord and so remember,
    All God's mercy to proclaim.
Who forgives all my transgressions,
    And with mercy gently heals;
Who redeems me from destruction,
    And with goodness kindly deals.

Working for those in oppression,
    God's own love and justice prove.
Slow to anger, full of mercy,
    Steadfast love our sins remove.
As the heav'ns are high above us,
    Vaster still God's love has been.
As the east from west is distant,
    So God puts away our sin.

As a father loves his children,
    God's compassion follows us.
Though we flourish and then wither,
    God remembers we are dust.
Though the wind blows o'er our living,
    Sweeping all our works away,
God's own covenant is stronger,
    Loving us beyond that day.

Unto all who keep the statutes,
    Steadfast in God's holy way;
Unto all who still remember
    God's commandments to obey;
To our children's children ever,
    God's own righteousness extends.
As it was in the beginning,
    God's love lasts, and never ends.

God's own throne is set in heaven,
    King o'er all the pow'rs of earth.
Ruling o'er the hosts of heaven,
    Lord of all who come to birth.
Bless the Lord now, every creature,
    All who live in God's control.
Join with us in songs and praises;
    Bless the Lord with heart and soul.

Psalm 103 is a meditation on God's goodness and steadfast love that is forgiving and everlasting. It starts with the psalmist calling upon himself to "Bless the Lord, O my soul, and all that is within me, bless God's holy name. Bless the Lord, O my soul, and forget not all God's benefits." The psalmist then lists the many ways God is good, merciful, gracious, and generous: forgiving iniquity, healing all our diseases, redeeming our lives from the Pit, crowning us with steadfast love and mercy, and satisfying us with good things as long as we live, so that our strength is renewed like a youth's. The psalm then turns to address the entire community, reflecting on the Lord's merciful and gracious nature. The Lord is slow to anger and abounding in steadfast love, removing our sin from us as far as the east is from the west. In spite of the fleeting nature of human life, God knows that we are dust and our days are short in the span of divine time. Yet, the Lord's steadfast love endures forever — from everlasting to everlasting. The psalm ends calling on all in heaven — God's angels and the heavenly hosts — to join in this song of blessing.

Psalm 104

8.7.8.7 D

HYMN OF JOY, RUSTINGTON *(preferred tune)*

Bless the Lord with all my being;
    Lord, my God, you have such might.
Cloaked with honor, grand and glorious,
    You are clothed with purest light.
Stretching out the heav'ns like tent cloth,
    You are chambered on the deep.
Riding on the wings of windstorm,
    Flame and fire your bidding keep.

Lord, you laid the earth's foundation,
    That it would be always sound.
By the word of your commanding,
    You set forth the ocean's bound.
Springs gush forth at your own bidding,
    Giving drink to every field.
Bird and beast and all your creatures,
    In that coolness find thirst healed.

Grass you cause to grow for cattle,
    Plants for us to cultivate.
Food you bring forth from our labor,
    Wine for joy and bread for plate.
Trees you give the birds for shelter,
    Mountain rock and cave for beast.
Sun and moon both mark the seasons;
    In their light we work and feast.

Lord, how great are all your workings;
    Wisdom marks them through and through.
All the earth is your possession;
    Great and small belong to you.

Food you give in each due season;
  At your hand come all good things.
By your Spirit you create us;
  Lord, your breath renewal brings.

May your glory reign forever.
  Lord, rejoice in all you make!
As you look on your creation,
  Mountains smoke, foundations shake.
May these words and thoughts be pleasing,
  For in you my joy is found.
Bless the Lord with all my being;
  With this song let praise abound.

Psalm 104 is a creation hymn and one of the "lodestones" of the psalter. It speaks not only of God's creative power, but also of God's saving power and purpose throughout the universe. Though other religions of the day had their own creation psalms, and this one shows some significant influence from the Egyptian hymn to the sun god Rah, what makes Israel's creation psalmody unique is that God is always at the center as creator and not dependent upon other factors, least of all, human intervention. What makes this psalm even more unique in the collection of creation hymns is that it is not anthropocentric — God does not create the world for human beings to be at the center of it. God fashions each element of the created order for its own distinct and unique purpose: streams to water trees, trees for birds to nest in, caves to shelter wild beasts, grass to feed cattle, etc. It celebrates the Lord as creator, ruler, savior, and sustainer of all that is, fashioned, governed, and sustained by the Lord's wisdom. The Lord opens his hand and gives all good things, especially life and breath, to all that live. Day is created for humans, night for wild animals. All have their place within the created order, parceled out by God's wisdom, which is visible throughout all of creation. Creation reveals the Lord's glory, which the psalmist sings to and prays will last forever. Everyone and everything has its appointed place — except the sinner. This is one of the most beautiful and comprehensive creation hymns in the entire psalter. In addition, remember, the creation narratives in Genesis were among the last to be written and were deeply influenced by psalms such as this one, as well as those that appear in the book of Job.

Psalm 105

Verses 1–11, 16–26, 37–45
CMD
GRATUS, SHEPHERD'S PIPES

We give you thanks, O Lord, our God!
    We call upon your name.
We must make known your mighty deeds
    To heal our people's pain.
This song of thanks and praise we raise
    To you, O living Lord.
And glory in your holy name;
    Your name be long adored!

We seek your presence and your strength,
    Your wondrous works of grace.
Your judgments and your miracles
    Are treasured in this place.
As Jacob's children, Abram's heirs,
    You chose us as your own.
With joyful hearts we seek you, Lord,
    To make your glory known.

You are the Lord, the living God,
    Whose judgments fill the earth.
Your covenant forever strong
    Is promise of true worth.
To Abraham and to his own
    You promised Canaan's land.
Your word is true, you make it good;
    On this our hopes still stand.

When famine spread across the land
    And left no bread or grain,
You sent a man ahead of them,

And Joseph was his name.
Though first enslaved, he spoke your word
    And soon he was set free
To serve the king in his own house
    As steward and trustee.

Then came his father Israel,
    An alien to that land.
But there you blessed and strengthened him,
    You led them by the hand.
Their foes dealt with them craftily
    And soon they were enslaved.
But you sent Moses back to them,
    And soon they would be saved.

You brought them out with wealth and gold,
    Surefooted, everyone.
Their foes were glad that they were gone,
    So dread had they become.
You spread your glory over them,
    A cov'ring for the day,
With fire to give them light by night
    And help them on their way.

They cried for food; you answered them
    With quail and heav'nly bread,
And water gushing from the rock,
    That filled a riverbed.
For Abram's sake you cared for them
    And gave them food and drink.
Your covenant is sure and true;
    From this you will not shrink.

You brought your people out with joy,
    Your chosen ones with song.
And gave to them the nations' lands;
    Their wealth to them was strong,

That they might keep your covenant,
  Its laws with one accord,
And serve you with their hearts and hands.
  Come now, and praise the Lord.

Psalm 105 is a psalm of praise that calls everyone to make known God's deeds among the people. The reading is divided, with the first six verses dominated by the language of praise — "Give thanks," "call," "sing," "glory," and "rejoice." Sing praise to him and speak of all his wonders. Seek the Lord and his strength continually. It then recounts the reasons for this praise: God's faithfulness to Israel, beginning with God's initial covenant with Abraham, Isaac, Jacob, Joseph, and the children of Israel — a covenant made forever — making them God's "chosen ones" with the promise of the land of Canaan as their inheritance. It then remembers their past: few in number and of little account and nomads in the land, often oppressed by the kings of other nations, and how God reproved their kings for his people's sake. They are, after all, the Lord's anointed ones — prophets who speak for the Lord. The famine that ultimately sent the children of Israel to Egypt is recalled. But for now, the focus is upon Joseph being sold into slavery, then imprisoned until the time that the Lord's word was to come to pass. (As the author of Hebrews reminds us, it can be a terrifying thing to fall into the hands of the Lord, as Joseph well learned! [Heb. 10:31]. How much have we attempted to domesticate the Lord for our own purposes?) But the Lord was faithful and the Pharaoh set Joseph free and made him lord of Pharaoh's house and ruler over all of his possessions, giving Joseph power to "imprison [Pharaoh's] princes at will in order to teach the Egyptian elders wisdom." There then follows a litany praising God for all that God has done among the children of Israel beginning with Abraham, through Joseph becoming Pharaoh's chief officer and lord of his household. That portion of the psalm remembers that, because of Joseph's success (and the famine), Israel came to Egypt and lived there as aliens. It was there that the Lord made the people very fruitful and strong — so much so that the Egyptians came to hate them. Then, God sent them Moses and Aaron and the plagues in Egypt to free the people. Following the ultimate woe — the striking down of all firstborn — God brought Israel out of Egypt with its silver and gold, so glad were the Egyptians to be rid of them, for dread of the Israelites had spread across Egypt. God spread the covering of fire by night and cloud by day to lead them. When asked, God fed them with quail and gave them bread from heaven, opened the rock to produce water in the wilderness, and did so because God remembered the covenant he had made with Abraham. The psalm concludes by remembering that God has brought the people out with joy and into the lands of the nations in Canaan. God gave them these lands and the wealth of all of their inhabitants, so that they might be a people who keep his statutes and observe his laws. The psalm ends with one final word of praise: "Hallelujah!"

Psalm 106

Verses 1–6, 19–23

8.7.8.7 D

BREWER, GLENDON, FABEN

Alleluia, Lord, we praise you!
    You are good; how good your ways!
Steadfast is your love forever;
    Who can utter all your praise?
Who can name your mighty doings;
    Who can fathom all your ways?
Blest are those who do your justice;
    Righteous always are their days.

Think of me, O Lord, remember,
    When you favor all your own.
Help me, Lord, when you deliver;
    Let your righteous way be known.
Let me know your prosp'rous favor,
    Shared by every chosen one.
Let me glory with your people,
    And rejoice in all you've done.

We have sinned like those before us,
    Generations, endlessly;
Doing wrong, pursuing evil,
    We have acted wickedly.
Calf of gold we formed at Horeb,
    Bowing down 'gainst your command,
Giving glory to an image,
    Made from metal by our hand.

They forgot you, God our Savior,
    All for them done by your hand:

159

Things you did for them in Egypt,
   Wondrous works in Pharaoh's land;
Awesome deeds of liberation,
   With their backs against the sea.
They forgot how oft you'd brought them
   From defeat to victory.

Thus you said you would destroy them,
   Render to them their own due,
Turn your wrath upon them fully,
   And destroy them through and through.
Had not Moses, your own chosen,
   Filled the breach, to calm your rage,
   Holy wrath would have consumed them,
   Wiping out their heritage.

P salm 106:1–18 seems to be a counterpoint to Psalm 105, which recounts all of God's acts on behalf of Israel from Abraham to their
entering the land of promise. Whereas Psalm 105 is silent on the people's
response, Psalm 106 is an extended confession of the people's faithless
response. Though it begins with the familiar refrain, "Hallelujah ['Praise
the Lord']! Give thanks to the Lord, for he is good; for his steadfast love
endures forever," it quickly turns into a corporate confession of sin, remembering the numerous ways the people have sinned, been stubborn
and untrusting in the face of God's steadfast love and care. "We and our
ancestors have sinned; we have committed iniquity, have done wickedly."
The recital of sins begins in Egypt, where they ignored God's wonderful
works. Liberated from Egypt, they rebelled against God at the Red Sea,
not trusting God to deliver them from the Egyptians. When God did save
them from their foe they rejoiced and sang God's praise, but then quickly
forgot God's works and counsel. Their cravings for food and water, their
murmurings and various rebellions in the wilderness, are recounted, and
Moses's intercession on their behalf, without which the Lord's wrath
would have destroyed all of them but Moses.

Psalm 107

8.7.8.7.8.8.7

NUN FREUT EUCH, MIT FREUDEN ZART

Verses 1–3, 17–22

We thank you, Lord, for you are good;
    Your love endures forever.
From east and west, from north and south,
    You call your own together.
Let all the Lord's redeemed sing praise;
    God's love endures beyond our days.
    Sing praise to our redeemer.

Though some were sick because of sin,
    And suffered much affliction,
They loathed the very thought of food,
    And begged for swift destruction.
Then unto you, they raised their cry;
    You sent your word, lest they should die.
    You healed them in their pleading.

Now let us thank the Lord our God,
    Whose love is steadfast ever.
God's wondrous works to humankind
    Are gifts beyond all measure.
This sacrifice of thanks and praise
    We sing in honor of your ways;
    Your love endures forever.

We thank you, Lord, for you are good;
   Your love endures forever.
From east and west, from north and south,
   You call your own together.
Let all the Lord's redeemed sing praise;
   God's love endures beyond our days.
   Sing praise to our redeemer.

Some wandered in the desert wastes;
   They could not find a city.
Hunger and thirst were all they knew;
   Their souls were faint with pity.
They cried to you in their distress;
   You brought them forth with faithfulness.
   Sing praise to our redeemer.

They thanked you, Lord, for you are good,
   Your steadfast love a wonder.
You satisfied their thirst with drink,
   With good things filled their hunger.
Let all the wise give ear, take heed;
   God's steadfast love fills every need.
   Sing praise to our redeemer.

Psalm 107 opens the fifth and last section of the psalter and is, suitably, a song of thanksgiving for the way God has delivered the people in times of trouble. It begins with the classic and oft-repeated phrase: "O give thanks to the Lord, for he is good; for his steadfast love endures forever." It then calls on the redeemed of the Lord to say so. The psalm then turns to describing those who have been so redeemed. It does not recount God's saving history with the nation. Rather, it focuses on God's redeeming actions with people in distress: the wandering hungry and thirsty ones with no place to rest; all those in prison's darkness, gloom, and depravity; those beset with illness, who could not eat and were near the gates of death; and those who were caught at sea during storms. Each section names God's saving action and then sings, "Let them thank the Lord for his steadfast love, for his wonderful works to humankind." It then challenges the people to extol the Lord's work among them, tell of God's saving deeds in the congregation, and offer thanksgiving sacrifices and songs of joy in the assembly of the elders.

Psalm 112

LM, *with refrains*
SACRED SONG

How blest are those who fear you, Lord,
Who praise your name with one accord,
Who take delight in your commands,
Their children mighty in the lands.

> *Refrain*:
> Come praise the Lord, come bless God's name;
> Sing "Hallelujah!" Spread God's fame.
> Come praise the Lord with all your might;
> Sing praise to God both day and night.

Their children grow in might and zest,
With wealth and riches they are blest.
Their righteousness is widely known,
A light in darkness for your own.
> *Refrain*

With gen'rous spirit do they lend,
Their grace and mercy without end;
Remembered for their lives approved,
The righteous will not e'er be moved.
> *Refrain*

No evil tidings do they fear,
Their lives in you, Lord, are secure.
Their hearts are steady, not brought low,
Victorious o'er their every foe.
> *Refrain*

Unto the poor they freely give;
Their righteousness shall ever live.
The wicked see with angry eye;
Their wants and lives will surely die.
    Refrain

Psalm 112 is a wisdom psalm — another acrostic — that sings the praises of those who fear the Lord. After an initial "Hallelujah," it lists the blessings ("happy are those") that come to those who delight in God's commandments. Descendants, wealth, riches, light come to those who are gracious, merciful, generous, and righteous. "They shall never be moved" is a biblical phrase that speaks of eternal blessing, and being remembered forever. They fear no evil tidings because their hearts are firm and secure in the Lord. In the end, they will look in triumph over their foes. They give freely, especially to the poor, and their righteousness endures forever. Their strength ("horn") is celebrated with honor. The wicked see it and are angry, gnash their teeth and melt away, and, in their desire, come to nothing.

Psalm 113

8.8.8.8.8.8

MELITA

Sing praises to the name of God;
    Come, servants now, and offer laud,
From this time forth and evermore,
    O'er all the world from shore to shore.
Blest is your name, O living Lord;
    O may your name be long adored.

You, Lord, are ruler of all lands;
    Their governments are in your hands.
There is no other like you, God;
    Your pow'r is great, your love is broad.
All you that live within God's pow'r,
    Sing praise in this and every hour.

You help the needy in distress;
    You give them life that conquers death.
You grant the homeless sheltered space,
    And fill the empty with your grace.
The great and small for you are one;
    In all things Lord, your will is done.

Come praise the Lord with all our breath,
    Who gives us vict'ry over death.
Praise to the Spirit who brings life,
    And nurtures us in every strife.
Praise Christ who conquers and is King,
    O Three in One, to you we sing.

P salm 113 is a psalm of praise that blesses God's name — "the Lord" — as sovereign of the entire earth, and calls upon all God's servants to praise the name of the Lord from "this time on and forevermore. From the rising of the sun to its setting the name of the Lord is to be praised." But the Lord is more than "high and mighty." And so, the psalmist asks, "Who is like the Lord our God . . . ," who though seated high above the heavens, nonetheless looks down from afar to raise the poor from the dust and the needy from the ash heap? The psalm continues to extol the Lord for his concern for all the creatures of his creation. Not only does the Lord come to its rescue, he makes the poor and needy sit with princes. The Lord has compassion on all in need and does something about it. God does this, not by bringing the mighty "low," as is the case in other places that extol the Lord for his concern for the poor and needy, but rather, by raising those in need to the status and conditions of nobility. He gives the barren woman both a home and children — a place to live in safety and a heritage to care for her in her days of need. Hallelujah!

Psalm 114

7.6.7.6 D

TOURS

When we came out of Egypt,
    That strange and cruel land,
As Jacob's own descendants,
    We left by your own hand.
And you, Lord, came out with us,
    To build yourself a home;
A holy, prized possession,
    A people for your own.

The waters saw you coming,
    As we approached the shore.
They fled to give us passage,
    So too at Jordan's door.
The mountains leaped before us,
    Like young and virile rams.
The hills skipped at our passing,
    Like flocks of playful lambs.

So tremble, stone and water,
    Before your face, O Lord.
You turn the rocks to water,
    The stones deep pools afford.
You travel still among us,
    To build yourself a home,
To make us your possession,
    A people for your own.

Psalm 114 is a hymn praising God's power and recounts the wonders God did in claiming the house of Israel as his own when bringing them out of Egypt to make them God's own dwelling place in the land of promise. The psalm uses various images from creation to emphasize God's sovereignty at critical points in Israel's life – the sea looked and fled; the river Jordan turned back to allow the people to cross over. At God's presence, the mountains skipped like rams and the hills like lambs. Why? Because it is the Lord, the one who turns rocks into pools of water and flint into a gushing spring, a reference to Moses striking the rock in the wilderness. The hymn is a remembrance of Israel's deliverance from Egypt and was later sung at Passover on the eighth day of that celebration, just as it still is today.

Psalm 116

CMD

FOREST GREEN, ALL SAINTS NEW

We love you Lord, for you have heard
    Our cries of deep distress;
You hear the anguish of our pleas,
    For this your name we bless.
Your name is merciful and right,
    And love shines from your face.
Ev'n in the lowest points of life,
    You guard us with your grace.

From death, from tears, from stumbling feet,
    You keep our lives secure;
While trust in others brings no help,
    With you we will not fear.
And so we set our feet to walk
    Your path within this land;
To follow you through any grief
    And trust your gracious hand.

What shall I give to you, O Lord,
    For all your good to me?
A gift that seeks for no reward,
    Except your face to see.
Salvation's cup in thanks we raise,
    And call upon your name.
O living Bread, receive our praise;
    Your presence now we claim.

Within this house we lift our hearts;
    Our lives we promise now.
This sacrifice of thanks and praise,
    Here, Lord, receive our vow.

As you have fed us in this place,
    Now lead us past these doors;
That all may learn to seek your face,
    And serve you evermore.

And so we set our feet to walk
    Your path within this land,
To follow you through any grief,
    And trust your gracious hand.
To you the maker of us all,
    To you the Risen Son,
To you the Spirit of new life,
    We lift our hearts in song.

Psalm 116 asks, "What shall we give to the Lord for all of God's goodness to us?" This psalm professes love for the Lord who hears our cries, who is gracious, righteous, and compassionate, and who preserves the simple (the naïve), who keeps our stumbling feet on God's path, preserving our lives. The psalmist had been surrounded by the snares of death; the pangs of dying were upon him as he suffered anguish and distress. As is often the case, the emotional side of his encounter with death was even more traumatic than the physical reality of it. In that anguish he called out to the Lord to save him and the Lord did. "What then," he asks, "shall I offer to the Lord in return for all of God's goodness?" The psalmist will lift the cup of salvation and call on the name of the Lord. He is promising to go to the temple to offer God a sacrifice of thanksgiving in the midst of God's people. The psalmist makes a final vow: "I am your servant, the child of your serving girl." He seals this promise with a pledge. Lifting the cup of salvation, in much the way we would offer a "toast" to another in tribute, he simply says, "Hallelujah!"

Psalm 118

Verses 1–2, 14–29

8.7.8.7 D, *with refrain*

To be sung to NARNIA *(© John Weaver); if the verses are divided in half, with the refrain forming either the first or last verse, the psalm can be sung to* ST. COLUMBA *or* EVAN

Refrain:
I thank you, Lord, for you are good,
    My God and sure Deliv'rer.
Your steadfast love and faithfulness,
    They shall endure forever.

You are my strength, my might, my hope,
    The source of my salvation.
Glad songs of victory are sung
    In righteous habitations.
Your right hand, it is valiant, Lord,
    Exalted in its working;
Your right hand is courageous, Lord,
    Undaunted and assuring.
    Refrain

I shall not die, yes, I will live,
    To tell again your story.
Recounting all that you have done,
    I'll sing your praise and glory.
You punished me in righteousness
    And did so most severely,
But did not give me up to death;
    You brought me forth in safety.
    Refrain

So open now these holy gates
    Wherein the righteous gather,
That I may enter and give thanks
    To you, my Lord and Savior.
For here I'll sing of steadfast love
    And pow'r beyond believing,
That conquers death and brings new life,
    Your love and grace revealing.
    Refrain

I give you thanks, you answered me;
    You are my sure salvation.
The one the builders cast aside,
    You've made the strong foundation.
This is your work, how marvelous!
    The gift of full redemption;
This is the day that you have made,
    A gift beyond description.
    Refrain

How blest are those who in your name
    Come to this place and gather,
Assembled in your holy name,
    To pray and sing together.
You are the Lord, the living God,
    Who gives us light as blessing.
With festal palm, with pipe and song,
    We gather here confessing:
    Refrain

Note: This psalm is appointed in two different configurations for Palm / Passion Sunday (vv. 1–2, 19–29), and for the Day of Resurrection (vv. 1–2, 14–24); both configurations are included below. Music available upon request; John Weaver may be contacted at marianneweaver@juno.com or through Andrew E. Henderson at aeh@mapc.com.

PALM / PASSION SUNDAY
Verses 1–2, 19–29

Refrain:
I thank you, Lord, for you are good,
    My God and sure Deliv'rer.
Your steadfast love and faithfulness,
    They shall endure forever.

Come, open now these holy gates
    Wherein the righteous gather,
That I may enter and give thanks
    To you, my Lord and Savior.
For here I'll sing of steadfast love
    And pow'r beyond believing,
That conquers death and brings new life,
    Your love and grace revealing.
    Refrain

I give you thanks, you answered me;
    You are my sure salvation.
The one the builders cast aside,
    You've made the strong foundation.
This is your work, how marvelous!
    The gift of full redemption;
This is the day that you have made,
    A gift beyond description.
    Refrain

How blest are those who in your name
    Come to this place and gather,
Assembled in your holy name,
    To pray and sing together.
You are the Lord, the living God,
    Who gives us light as blessing.
With festal palm, with pipe and song,
    We gather here confessing:
    Refrain

Day of Resurrection

Refrain:
I thank you, Lord, for you are good,
    My God and sure Deliv'rer.
Your steadfast love and faithfulness,
    They shall endure forever.

You are my strength, my might, my hope,
    The source of my salvation.
Glad songs of victory are sung
    In righteous habitations.
Your right hand, it is valiant, Lord,
    Exalted in its working.
Your right hand is courageous, Lord,
    Undaunted and assuring.
    Refrain

I shall not die, yes, I will live,
    To tell again your story.
Recounting all that you have done,
    I'll sing your praise and glory.
You punished me in righteousness
    And did so most severely,
But did not give me up to death;
    You brought me forth in safety.
    Refrain

Come, open now these holy gates
    Wherein the righteous gather,
That I may enter and give thanks
    To you, my Lord and Savior.
For here I'll sing of steadfast love
    And pow'r beyond believing,
That conquers death and brings new life,
    Your love and grace revealing.
    Refrain

I give you thanks, you answered me;
　You are my sure salvation.
The one the builders cast aside,
　You've made the strong foundation.
This is your work, how marvelous!
　The gift of full redemption;
This is the day that you have made,
　A gift beyond description.
　Refrain

Psalm 118 opens with the familiar words: "Give thanks to the Lord, for he is good; his steadfast love endures forever!" With these words the psalmist — possibly the king — calls the people to a hymn of praise that remembers the ways God has blessed and intervened on his behalf. The Lord has responded to the psalmist's distress and so he confesses, "The Lord is with me, I will not fear; what can man do to me?" Consequently, he can look at his enemies with satisfaction; the Lord is among those who support him. Therefore, it is better to take refuge in the Lord than in men, in the Lord than in princes. The king now reflects that though the nations surrounded him to destroy him, in the name of the Lord he cut them off. He was pushed violently to the point of falling, but the Lord intervened. At this we have a psalm within a psalm — the king's own words of praise directed to the Lord. "The Lord is my strength and my song; he has become the source of my salvation. There are glad songs of victory in the tents of the righteous." In victorious joy he continues, "I shall not die, but I shall live to tell of the works of the Lord. He punished me severely, but did not give me over to death." Herein, the early church heard the words of Christ speaking to them in and through the psalm, which is why it is appointed both for Palm Sunday and Easter Day liturgies. Finally, the psalmist prepares to go to the temple to pay his vows: "Open to me the gates of righteousness, that I may enter through them and pay my vow. This is the gate of the Lord, only the righteous shall enter through it. The stone which the builders rejected has become the chief corner stone. This is marvelous in our eyes." Again, phrase after phrase of this psalm has worked itself into the treasury of the Gospels and Christian prayer. "This is the day the Lord has made, let us rejoice and be glad in it." The people shout, "Save us, we beseech you, O Lord (Hosanna!)" as Jesus rides into Jerusalem. "Blessed is the one who comes in the name of the Lord." All of this is the language of the worshiper in the temple, confessing loyalty and trust in God: "You are my God, and I will give thanks to you; you are my God, I will extol you." The prayer concludes as it began: "O give thanks to the Lord, for he is good, for his steadfast love endures forever."

Psalm 119:1–16

CM

SOHR

Blest are the uncorrupt in heart,
    Whose ways are right and true,
Who never from your law depart,
    But ever fly to you.

Blest are all those who keep your word,
    And practice your commands,
Who with their hearts still seek you, Lord,
    And serve you with their hands.

Great hope we find within your law,
    Thus firm our lives are bound.
When trials, troubles, hurts arise,
    In you true life is found.

Then do we sing with deepest joy
    The honor of your name.
For when your statutes we obey,
    Our lives are kept from shame.

To you, O God of Truth and Law,
    To you, O living Word,
To you, O Comforter of life,
    May now our praise be heard.

P salm 119 is the longest psalm in the entire collection of 150 (151 if you are Roman Catholic), and the longest chapter in the entire Bible. It is an acrostic poem: each eight-line stanza starts with a letter of the Hebrew alphabet, beginning with the first (*Alef*), and continuing in order to the last (*Tav*). The central theme is praise for God's Law (*Torah*), and though it contains mini-psalms of praise, petition, lament, meditation, trust, and confidence, it is, in the whole, a wisdom psalm captured by "Blessed are those who walk in the law of the Lord; they are blameless!" (The NRSV's "Happy" is also a fair translation of the Hebrew, but far weaker, as "blessed" has the connotation of it being something received rather than created.) And so the psalmist continues by asking for God's help in keeping God's way. For the psalmist's part, God's words are treasures that will be committed to memory, so they may be deeply embedded in the heart, quick to come to his lips, always available for meditation, and never to be forgotten. But such discipline was no more easily achieved or sought then than now. We could do worse than spend time memorizing portions of scripture; they might become our counselors. Loss of the pedagogy of memorizing scripture has left us a church that is biblically illiterate. Little wonder, then, that our values, even in the church, are shaped by a culture of consuming and competing, where success is valued more than faithfulness.

Psalm 119:33–40

CM

KEDDY

Teach me, O Lord, your statutes' ways;
    I'll keep them to the end.
True understanding give my heart;
    Your ways I will defend.

In your commandments, lead me, Lord;
    In them my footsteps train.
Turn now my heart to your decrees,
    And not to selfish gain.

From vain things turn away my eyes;
    Give life and strength each day.
Confirm to all who fear your name
    The goodness of your way.

Now turn away the scorn I dread;
    Your judgments, they suffice.
Revive me in your righteousness;
    In justice give me life.

V erses 33–40 appear in the second portion of this, the longest psalm in the Bible, a wisdom psalm composed using the acrostic pattern. The theme of remaining in "the way" of the Lord dominates this portion, with the psalmist praying "teach me your statutes. Make me understand the way of your precepts." As the psalmist's soul melts away in sorrow, she pleads for God's word to strengthen her and put false and vain ways far away from her. She speaks of clinging to God's decrees lest she be put to shame. The psalm is filled with rich liturgical language: "Teach me, O Lord, the way of your statutes, and I will observe it to the end." This theme is repeated in various expressions, using verbs like "lead," "turn," "confirm," and culminating in the psalmist reminding God that she has longed for his precepts and is pleading for God to save her from scorn and revive her in God's righteousness.

Psalm 119:97–104

CMD

HALIFAX, FOREST GREEN, ELLECOMBE, KINGSFOLD

Lord, your commandment makes me wise;
    Oh, how I love your law!
I mediate upon your words;
    In them there is no flaw.
Both day and night I think on them;
    Their wisdom is so sure.
They make me wiser than my foes;
    They ever shall endure.

My teachers' wisdom is surpassed
    By these your fine decrees.
My understanding is far more
    In kind and in degree.
More than an elder or a sage,
    Their wisdom is supreme.
In your commandments there is truth,
    To keep life strong and clean.

I keep my step from evil's way,
    To hold fast to your word.
I turn not from your ordinance;
    Your teachings I have heard.
How sweet are they within my mouth,
    Like honey on my tongue.
Your precepts are unlike all else;
    All others I will shun.

P salm 119:97–104 continues its acrostic and starts with a statement of how the psalmist loves God's Law. Following the injunction of Psalm 1, the psalmist meditates on it day and night. It makes him wiser than his enemies and gives him more understanding than his teachers or his elders. It keeps his feet in check and is sweeter on his tongue than honey. God's precepts are unlike any other; therefore, he hates every other way.

Psalm 119:105–112

10.10.10.10

TOULON

Your word, O Lord, is light upon my path,
A lantern shining truth to guide my ways.
An oath I've sworn, this vow I now confirm:
To keep your righteous statutes all my days.

Though I'm afflicted and worn down with pain,
As you have promised, give me life anew.
Receive this off'ring of my thanks and praise!
Teach me your way and keep my footsteps true.

Though life is fragile and within my hands,
Your law remains my constant trust and stay.
Though many snares the wicked lay for me,
I have not turned aside from your own way.

Your laws are my eternal heritage;
They are pure joy, their words my heart's delight.
I am resolved to follow your commands,
To walk forever by your word's true light.

This portion of Psalm 119 begins with the well-known words, "Your word is a lamp to my feet and a light to my path," and then takes up the theme of fulfilling the vow that has been taken to study it. Yet, as he does, he finds himself severely afflicted and prays for relief. Though he holds his life in his hands — is responsible for it on a day-to-day basis and finds it fragile — his enemies continue to beset him, setting snares for him. Yet, he does not turn aside or forget God's law. He is resolved to maintain his vow to follow God's commands, for they are his heritage and the joy of his heart.

Psalm 121

CM

DUNDEE

We lift our eyes unto the hills;
    Where shall our help find birth?
Our help comes from the living God,
    Who made the heav'ns and earth.

You will not let our feet be moved;
    Our lives shall long endure.
With constant watch and sleepless eye,
    You keep us all secure.

You safely shade from evil's work;
    Your care is all around.
No force on earth — not sun nor moon —
    Has pow'r to strike us down.

O Lord, you guard us all our days,
    Protecting in our strife,
Our going out, our coming in,
    Both now and all through life.

Psalm 121 was sung by pilgrims making their way to the temple to worship. Lifting their eyes to the hills (remember, Jerusalem is the highest mountain in that part of the land), they reaffirm that help comes only from the Lord, the maker of heaven and earth. He shall assure their security, keep them established, and ensure that their feet do not slip from the path. For the Lord never slumbers or sleeps but is ever watchful, a shade on their right hand; the sun shall not smite them by day nor the moon by night. The Lord shall keep them and guard their coming and going, both now and forever.

Psalm 122

10.10.10.10

TOULON

Glad was my heart when they said unto me,
Come now with us the Lord's own house to see.
So now my feet are standing in your gate,
City of God, Jerusalem the great.

Built as God's city safe upon a hill,
There all the tribes by God's decree come still,
And in these walls so strong and now restored,
Gather to bless and praise the living Lord.

High on the throne of judgment sits the king,
Ruling in justice, David's peace to bring;
Bringing true justice and God's own accord,
Life, hope, and peace to all who serve the Lord.

Pray for the peace of God's Jerusalem,
Peace to these walls and all who dwell therein.
May all who come here flourish and increase,
And in God's house find life and perfect peace.

186

Psalm 122 is one that was sung by visitors as they made their way to Jerusalem and the temple for one of their pilgrimage festivals. It identifies Jerusalem as built and established by God and its temple as God's dwelling place. Its plaintive plea, "Pray for the peace of Jerusalem," has been answered by innumerable pilgrims to this very day, and is as important now as it has ever been. May all who love that Jerusalem — Jew, Christian, and Muslim — prosper, continue to pray for the city's peace, and learn to live together, there and everywhere, in the security of that peace.

Psalm 123

7.6.7.6 D

ES FLOG EIN KLEINS WALDVÖGELEIN, LLANGLOFFAN,

JONATHAN'S TUNE *(preferred tune)*

To you enthroned in heaven,
    To you we turn our eye,
Like servants with their masters,
    As maids to mistress sigh.
To you we look, O Lord God,
    Our master in the heav'ns,
Until you give us mercy,
    Until our hardship ends.

Have mercy on us, Lord God,
    Your mercy to us send,
For we have known contempt, Lord,
    Derision without end.
Our souls are overburdened
    By scorn from those at ease,
Who heap contempt upon us
    While doing as they please.

Have mercy on us, Lord God,
    Have mercy without end.
Look down on us in pity,
    Your great compassion send.
Our eyes look to you only,
    For mercy and release.
You are the Lord Most Holy;
    In mercy, give us peace.

P salm 123 is the plea of a supplicant coming before the Lord in humility, asking for God's gracious mercy in helping her contend with the scorn and contempt of her enemies. Notice that it is titled "A Song of Ascents," meaning it was used by pilgrims approaching Jerusalem to worship in the temple. As the eyes of servants look to the hand of their master, and as the eyes of a maid look to the hand of her mistress for help, so the psalmist looks to the Lord for mercy amid the abuse and degradations of the proud. Those who live in ease not only remain oblivious to the psalmist's need but actually blame her for it as justification for their doing nothing to help. Does that sound familiar?

Psalm 125

CM

DUNLAP'S CREEK, ST. PETER

How firm are those who trust the Lord,
    Like Zion's lofty mount;
They stand secure, shall not be moved,
    Their days beyond all count.

As mountains guard Jerusalem,
    The Lord so guards us all,
A circling pow'r of faithfulness
    That shall not let us fall.

The scepter of great wickedness
    Shall not possess God's land,
Allotted to the chosen ones;
    In righteousness they stand.

Do good unto the good, O Lord,
    Those upright in their hearts.
Turn back the wicked on themselves
    To taste their evil arts.

Bring peace unto Jerusalem,
    To Israel, shalom.
Sustain all those who trust in you,
    And claim them as your own.

189

Psalm 125 is a song of ascents, and less a prayer than a wisdom hymn that extols the Lord's ability to care for those who trust in him. Like Mt. Zion, they will not be moved. Like the mountains that surround Mt. Zion, so the Lord surrounds his people, and will do so forever. Reigns of wickedness shall not fall on the land that has been allotted to the righteous, that they may not stretch out their hand and do wrong. Finally, there is the petition: "Do good, O Lord, to those who are good," followed by the parallel refrain, "and to those who are upright in their hearts." But for those who turn aside to walk in their own way, the Lord will lead them away with the other evildoers. The psalm ends by invoking peace on Jerusalem, not unlike our politicians invoking God's blessing on America.

Psalm 126

CM

ST. PETER, MCKEE

When God arose to bring us home,
    Our lives were like a dream.
Our mouths were filled with shouts of joy;
    With laughter did we sing.

The nations said among themselves,
    "For them God's done great things."
Great things indeed you've done, O Lord,
    And so to you we sing.

May those who sow in tears of pain
    Reap joy, and find life good.
Though we set out with burdened hearts,
    You bring us home renewed.

Psalm 126 is another pilgrim song, one of the songs of ascents sung by worshipers as they made their way to the temple. It remembers the initial joy experienced by the people upon their return home to Jerusalem from the Babylonian exile. They were like those who dream: their mouths were filled with laughter, their tongues with shouts of joy. As the Lord had promised, the nations said among themselves, "The Lord has done great things for them." In affirmation the worshipers declare it themselves: "The Lord has done great things for us," and in them they rejoice. They have been saved. But now home, there are new challenges. The second half of the psalm falls into a petition for God to bless them, to come and restore their fortunes, like water rushing through the watercourses in the Negeb. When the rain comes, those flat, dry riverbeds suddenly become awash with torrents of water. May the restoration come as suddenly, so that those who sow in tears may reap in joy. Planting season in the ancient Near East was associated with sorrow for many reasons, not the least being that the summer drought was drawing near and threatening to destroy the seed — the last they had. May they reap with shouts of joy because the crop has been abundant beyond belief.

Psalm 127

LM

BRESLAU

Unless our house is built by God,
The work we do will bring no gain.
Unless God keeps the city safe,
The sentries keep alert in vain.

How false it is to work all day,
From dawn into the dark of night.
Lord, you provide for those you love,
And give them rest as your delight.

Our children are a gift from God,
A source of comfort and increase.
They shall defend against our foes,
To bring us strength and days of peace.

Psalm 127 reminds us that the Lord is our builder and maker, and unless the Lord builds the house, those who build it labor in vain. So too for the city, and so too for those who go to bed late and rise early, working 24/7 and eating the bread of anxious toil. It is all vanity! Now the psalm shifts from the things we anxiously try to do to make a name for ourselves, to God's gifts of heritage — that is, our children. They are like arrows in the hands of a warrior. Here, there is a double entendre that we miss when paraphrasing "son" to "children" for the sake of inclusivity. The image of arrow connotes both sexual potency that continues to maintain the tribe and the protection that a large family provides. Might "quiver full of them" also be a reference to a wife's womb, which was believed to hold those children before conception? In any case, happy are those who have a household full of them. However, at the end of the day, it is not the presence of many children that brings prosperity and protection. That comes from the Lord. For unless the Lord builds our house, all else that we try to do is in vain.

Psalm 128

CM

WINCHESTER OLD, TALLIS' ORDINAL

How blest are those who fear the Lord,
    Who walk in God's own ways.
The fruit of labor from your hands
    Shall be yours all your days.

You shall be happy, filled with good;
    It shall go well with you.
How blest are those who fear the Lord,
    Whose ways are good and true.

Your spouse will be a fruitful vine,
    The comfort of your home.
Your children, olive shoots will be,
    Abundant and well grown.

From Zion God will bless your life;
    May all your days go well!
Your children's children may you see!
    Peace be on Israel!

Psalm 128 is titled "A Song of Ascents," which tells us it was part of an entrance liturgy to the temple that was employed as people made their three annual compulsory visits to Jerusalem to worship during one of the three major feasts. It is a wisdom psalm whose message is very much like Psalm 1: those who walk in God's ways receive God's blessing — the negative is not even considered! It may have been offered by the pilgrims themselves, or it may have been invoked on the pilgrims as they entered the temple. But, whereas Psalm 1 is general in its application, this one is more personal, expressing the blessings and their impact on one's spouse and children. It concludes with a series of general blessings, first on the pilgrim worshiper, then on Jerusalem, and finally on all of Israel itself.

Psalm 130

8.7.8.7 D

IN BABILONE

From the depths of deepest grieving,
    Lord, I cry to you in trust.
If you counted our transgressions,
    Who could be considered just?
But with you is sure forgiveness,
    Mercy full, beyond belief.
Here I stand, prepared to serve you,
    Filled with reverence and belief.

Eagerly I wait before you,
    List'ning for your voice, O Lord.
As a watchman longs for morning,
    So I long to hear your word.
Trust the Lord, now, all you people;
    God's love gives us life anew,
Saving us from all transgression,
    With a love both strong and true.

Psalm 130 is a classic lament for those living "in the depths" of life, whether physical or emotional, waiting on God to come and save. Notice that it is also a "psalm of ascents." It is being used by a pilgrim who has come to the temple in Jerusalem to worship God in the midst of despair. Out of the depths he has been crying to the Lord, with no response. Now he pleads again for the Lord to hear his voice and supplication. Notice that the psalmist has moved beyond self-recrimination. This is about more than personal sin. The pit is not God's punishment, for if God counted sin and thus punished, who would stand? No one — we would all find ourselves in the pit of God's judgment! No; with God there is always forgiveness. And so, the psalmist continues to hold tenaciously to God's word and wait and watch with an intensity that exceeds that of the watchmen waiting for the morning. The psalmist knows that when God comes, it will be with steadfast love, healing, and redemption. He prays, "Come, Lord; redeem all Israel!" This is a prayer for all who wrestle with depression, all with chronic or terminal illness, all who spend sleepless nights in anxiety and worry, and for any who find themselves in the pit of life for whatever reason.

Psalm 131

Verses 1–3

II.II.II.II

To be sung to I WONDER AS I WANDER *by J. J. Niles*

My heart is not proud nor my eye set too high;
My time is not spent on things higher than I,
But like a weaned child in its mother's embrace,
My soul rests secure in this calm, quiet place.

O Israel, hope in the Lord evermore,
Who comforts our soul and our spirit restores.
And as a weaned child knows its mother is true,
Our hearts and our eyes, Lord, look only to you.

Psalm 131, though brief, is lovely and filled with quiet confidence in God's ability and commitment to care. Its female imagery suggests that its author may have been a woman. It gives us a wonderful and lyric picture of someone who knows that pride leads to a fall, and contemplation of matters beyond one's capacity for understanding leads to frustration at best and anguish, doubt, and even denial, at worst. Rather, she calms and quiets her soul, like a weaned child does, resting securely in her mother's embrace. So too, she will do what she calls all Israel to do: hope in the Lord, and rest in God's embrace.

Psalm 132

7.6.7.6 D

JONATHAN'S TUNE, LLANFYLLIN

O Lord, remember David,
    The hardship he endured,
The vow he swore before you,
    The vow, O Lord, you heard:
"My house I will not enter,
    Nor rest myself afford,
Until I find a sure place,
    A dwelling for the Lord."

In Ephrathah we heard it;
    Word ran throughout the land.
In Jaar's fields we found it;
    The ark therein did stand.
Thus now we seek your dwelling,
    Our worship to afford,
To bow before your footstool,
    And praise you, living Lord.

Rise up, O Lord, and go forth
    To your own resting place,
You and your ark of presence,
    Your mercy seat of grace.
Your priests be clothed in justice,
    And joy your faithful's way.
For David's sake, we pray you,
    Turn not your face away.

You swore an oath to David,
    A promise he did own:
"A son from your own body
    Will sit upon your throne.

If they will keep my cov'nant
  And heed my own decrees,
Their sons shall also follow,
  His throne theirs too shall be."

You, Lord, have chosen Zion
  As your own dwelling place.
It is your home forever;
  You bless it with your grace.
You grant us great abundance;
  Salvation clothes each priest.
Your faithful stand before you
  In joy that will not cease.

Remember, Lord, your promise,
  For David's sake alone:
"A horn for him will sprout up,
  And occupy his throne.
A lamp for my anointed
  From which my light will stream.
Disgrace shall clothe his rivals,
  While his own crown will gleam."

Psalm 132 is a royal psalm that celebrates and legitimates the reign of the Davidic dynasty, recalling the covenant the Lord made with David to ensure his reign as well as that of his descendants on the throne of all Israel forever (2 Samuel 7). It begins recalling David's hardships in capturing Jerusalem to establish there a capital for a united kingdom, then his vow to build a temple so that the Lord would have a resting place among them. "We heard of it in Ephrathah; we found it in the fields of Jaar," is a reference to the return of the Ark of the Covenant, which had been lost in battle to the Philistines but was left in the field of Jaar because it was perceived as too dangerous (1 Sam. 6:1–7:2) until David brought it to Jerusalem and placed it in the tent of meeting he had erected there (2 Samuel 6). With the ark in Jerusalem, the city was considered the place of the Lord's habitation, until the division of the kingdom after Solomon's rule. The psalm includes a remembrance of God's oath to David that one of his sons would always sit on the throne, and the promise that the Lord, not David, had chosen Zion as his "desired habitation" forever. It concludes by reciting the blessings that come to Jerusalem because of God's presence there, and how God will continue to bless the descendants of David who sit on his throne (cause a horn to sprout up for David).

Psalm 133

CM

CRIMMOND, BEATITUDO

Behold the goodness of our Lord;
How blest it is to be
A company of God's beloved,
In holy unity.

Like precious oil upon the head,
A healing for our strife,
It flows throughout our common bond,
Refreshing all of life.

As dew on Zion's mountaintop
Brings freshness to its door,
Our Lord commands life in our midst,
And brings it evermore.

Psalm 133 sings of the blessings of unity among all God's people: "How good it is when brothers and sisters dwell in unity together." The psalm of blessing, again, a psalm of ascents being sung as pilgrims make their way to Jerusalem, describes the blessings of harmony and concord among the people, whether within the immediate family, the clan, or the nations, especially as they make their way to Mount Zion. Such unity is good and pleasant, and like precious, fragrant oil. Oil was used in biblical times for healing wounds, as a cosmetic on skin and hair, and for anointing kings, priest, and prophets. Such oil of blessing is poured in abundance in Jerusalem like the dew of Mount Hermon, and runs down upon the beard and over the collar and onto the robe. The image of Aaron refers to the priesthood in Jerusalem; for it is there that the Lord "commanded" his blessing ("ordained" is too weak) — life forevermore. The pilgrimage formed a bond of blessing itself, not unlike contemporary pilgrimages to holy places, with the ultimate blessing coming upon entering the temple. This psalm has had a rich liturgical life in the church, often used in calling people to the Lord's Table. Augustine used it as warrant for the development of monastic communities who were brotherhoods in which such unity was to dwell.

Psalm 134

CM

AZMON, SPOHR

O bless the Lord with joyful song;
    Sing hymns of pow'r and fame,
All people who within this house
    Are gathered in God's name.

Come lift your hands within this place,
    Where burn the sacred signs,
And pray that now our Lord's own face
    O'er all the earth may shine.

From Zion, from this holy hill,
    O Lord, our Maker, send
The holy knowledge of your will,
    Salvation without end.

Psalm 134 is the last "Song of Ascents," and concludes the section of such psalms that began with Psalm 120. It is short and is both a call to worship and a word of blessing. Some think it is a liturgical blessing that was invoked upon a new "shift" of priests coming to take up their service in the temple, a charge and blessing on the "changing of the guard" within the temple personnel. Others think it is simply a word of priestly blessing invoked over pilgrims as they come to the temple to bless God, make sacrifice, and dwell, for a time, in the presence of the Lord. Its tri-form structure is built around the invitation to "Come, bless the Lord," "Lift up your hands" (the posture of prayer), and the priestly blessing: "May the Lord, maker of heaven and earth, bless you from Zion." Zion, of course, is God's holy mountain, Jerusalem, but also a reference to the temple which was at the very top of the mountain and understood to be the Lord's dwelling place on earth, or, better, the "thin place" where heaven and earth met.

Psalm 137

11.8.11.8 D

SAMANTHRA

By Babylon's rivers we gathered to meet
   And in great despair we all wept,
Remembering Zion, your most holy hill,
   The place where our hopes were all kept.
When asked to sing praises of Zion, our home,
   And lift up our voices in song,
On limbs of the willows we hung up our harps
   In protest defiant and strong.

Lord, how could we lift up our voices in song,
   To praise you in this foreign land?
If ever Jerusalem I should forget,
   Then wither and blight my right hand!
And let my tongue cling to the roof of my mouth,
   Should I not remember that place,
Jerusalem, city of my highest joy,
   The home of the God of all grace.

Remember, O Lord, on the day that it fell,
   Our neighbors who helped tear it down,
How they came to sack and did shout in great joy:
   "Tear down; burn it all to the ground."
O Babylon, great is your pow'r to destroy,
   Such conquering havoc you wage.
How happy are those whose revenge pays you back
   By striking your children in rage.

By Babylon's rivers in exile we weep,
   And filled with repentance we pray:
Forgive the transgressions that drive us from home

And bring us harsh judgment each day.
Restore us, O Lord, bring us back to your land,
And there we will serve you alone!
We'll take up our harps then and sing this new song:
"Jerusalem, our common home."

Psalm 137 is an imprecatory psalm of lament that was composed during the Babylonian exile (587–540 BCE) while the Jews who had been deported there remembered Jerusalem. Their captors tormented them by asking them to sing the pilgrimage psalms of ascents they had sung as they made their way to the temple, which now no longer existed. It had been totally destroyed by the Babylonians in the sack of Jerusalem. This is the equivalent of asking a conquered people to sing their national anthem to their conquerors, bringing humiliation to the captives. In defiance, the psalmist responds, "How can we sing the Lord's song in a foreign land?" But refusing to sing does not mean forgetting, and so a vow is taken to never forget what has happened. While remembering their captivity and exile and Jerusalem's destruction, the psalmist also invokes a curse on those who destroyed the city and put them in bondage, not only the Babylonians but also the Edomites — Jerusalemites' neighbors who were descendants of Jacob's disinherited brother, Esau (Gen. 27:1–40). The Edomites acted out the ancient hatred between Esau and Jacob by helping the Babylonians destroy Jerusalem. Here is where most readings or settings for this psalm stop, and in doing so they sidestep the curse invoked in verses 8 and 9. These startling words of imprecation against Babylon and Edom invoke destruction, not only upon the city, but also upon the city's children. Often, those who designed lectionaries put these final verses in brackets, as if to avoid them. However, it was Dietrich Bonhoeffer who insisted that the psalm be prayed in its fullness. Sitting in his Nazi cell, awaiting execution, he observed that praying this psalm somehow brought him peace, allowing him to hand over to God all desire for vengeance.

Psalm 138

CM

GRAFENBERG, WEST END

Give thanks to God with all our hearts;
    Sing praises filled with fame.
Bow down in this the Lord's own house,
    And bless God's holy name.

We bless you for your steadfast love,
    For faith strong as a beam.
Your holy name and living Word
    Stand over all supreme.

We call to you for daily strength,
    Your answer swift and true.
Our lives find strength, our hearts new hope,
    And faith is born anew.

All leaders, monarchs, presidents,
    You by your word reprove.
You shelter all the poor and weak,
    And all the proud remove.

Though troubles fill our daily lives,
    Your work through them is shown
To have a purpose of your own;
    In love you bring us home.

Psalm 138 is a psalm of thanksgiving that celebrates the Lord's intervention on the psalmist's behalf. The language is rich in the action of praise and worship, and the recognition that in all of this God has again demonstrated his steadfast love and faithfulness — the qualities that most regularly describe the Lord in the psalter. Thereby, the Lord has again exalted his own name. The psalmist called and the Lord answered, increasing the strength of the supplicant's soul. The psalm is attributed to David, and clearly has royal overtones as it notes that all the kings of the earth shall praise the Lord, for they have heard the words of God's mouth. They too shall sing of the ways of the Lord. Though high, the Lord regards the lowly, but the haughty God perceives from far away — keeps them at arm's length but still under surveillance! As God has cared for and intervened in the past, so God shall continue to do so. Consequently, the psalmist confesses, "Though I walk in the midst of trouble, you preserve me against the wrath of my enemies." The psalm ends with a final affirmation of security: "the Lord will fulfill his purpose for me." Then, confessing that God's steadfast love endures forever, there is one final plea: "Do not forsake me, for I am but the work of your hands."

Psalm 139

Verses 1–6, 13–18

LM

ST. CRISPIN *(preferred tune)*

Lord, you have searched and seen me through.
Your eye commands with piercing view
My rising and my resting hours,
My heart and flesh with all their powers.

Within your circling love I stand;
On every side I find your hand.
Awake, asleep, at home, abroad,
Your breath sustains me, living God.

Could I so false, so faithless be,
To quit your service, turn, and flee?
Where, Lord, could I your presence shun,
Or from your mighty glory run?

Or should I try to hide from sight
Beneath a covering veil of night?
One glance from you, one piercing ray,
Would kindle darkness into day.

Your Spirit, Lord, called me to birth.
You brought me living from the earth.
You know my being through and through.
Lord, keep me ever near to you.

Psalm 139 explores the wonder and marvelous nature of God with us, who knows us through and through, who loves and cares for us, and whose presence is closer to us than we are to ourselves. It is one of the most beautiful, intimate prayers in the entire Psalter. There is nothing we can do or say that the Lord does not know. "Even before a word is on my tongue, O Lord, you know it completely." God surrounds us and holds us. There is nowhere we can go or ever find ourselves that God is not also present with us, his hand leading, his right hand holding us fast. "Such knowledge is too wonderful for me; it is so high that I cannot attain it." It has been thus from our very beginnings, when God was forming our inward parts, knitting us together in our mother's womb. Reflecting on the miracle of who we are — "fearfully and wonderfully made" — the psalmist stands in awe and wonder. God has known us and has had our days written in his book before the first of them came to be — an expression of the wondrous wisdom and knowledge of God, not a fatalistic notion of human life. God's ways are so vast they cannot be counted. And suppose they could, God would still be there: "I am still with you." The prayer closes with a curse, not included here, that makes many uncomfortable. But if you read it carefully, it is a calling of God's vengeance on the wicked, the bloodthirsty and malicious who lift themselves against God and God's ways. He reminds the Lord that he — the psalmist — hates those who hate God, and loathes those who rise up against God and God's ways. God's enemies are the psalmist's enemies, so much so, that he hates them with a "perfect hatred." In these days when mass shootings, the abuse of police power, and the use of torture in pursuit of security have revealed our national hypocrisy concerning human rights, perhaps we too can offer these words as an expression of our horror at those who have betrayed us, for whatever reason, and invoke God's curse on such behavior. The psalm ends in the wonder with which it began: "Search me, O God, and know my heart; test me and know my thoughts. See if there is any wicked way in me, and lead me in the way that is everlasting."

Psalm 141

7.6.7.6 D

MUNICH, EIGHTH DAY

I call upon your name, Lord;
    Make haste to answer me.
Hear now my supplication,
    And listen to my plea.
I offer here my praises,
    Like incense sweet and strong.
And lift my hands before you,
    In prayers of evensong.

Keep guard upon my mouth, Lord;
    Watch o'er the words I speak.
Keep back my heart from evil,
    Nor let me vengeance seek.
The smoothness of those ways, Lord,
    Will leave my life bereft.
O hear my prayer and save me
    From wickedness and death.

Your word, O Lord, is righteous;
    Your ways are just and true.
You scatter evildoers,
    And smash their works in two.
So keep my eyes upon you,
    Safe from their traps and snares.
You are my only refuge,
    My strength in all life's cares.

Psalm 141 is a wisdom psalm that is a personal petition and calls on God for protection from the lures of evil. It alternates between "the way of life" and "the way of death" — the traditional "two ways" theme of wisdom literature. It opens with a call to prayer that has, ever after, been used in communities gathered for evening prayer: "Let my prayer rise before you as incense, the lifting up of my hands as an evening sacrifice." It recalls the incense burning in the temple as a symbol of the prayers of the faithful. God is called upon to "set a guard over my mouth, and keep watch over the door of my lips. Do not turn my heart to any evil." God is asked to keep the psalmist from the company of those who work iniquity. "Do not let me eat of their delicacies." It is a plea to be kept from the company of those who walk in the way of evil and, rather, to be kept in the way of good, even to the point of saying, "Let the righteous strike me. . . ." This is an expression of continual openness to correction on the way, especially by those who are wiser than oneself. This is followed by the plea that "the oil of the wicked never anoint my head." The imagery quickly shifts to violence that befits the wicked. But, just as quickly, the psalmist returns her focus upon the Lord and addresses God directly: "O God, my Lord; in you I seek refuge; do not leave me defenseless. Keep me from the trap that the wicked have laid for me; let them fall into their own nets, while I escape."

Psalm 145

10.10.10.10

ELLERS, TOULON, NATIONAL HYMN, WOODLANDS

Verses 1–5, 17–21

We will extol you, Lord, our God and King,
And bless your name forever without end.
With each new day your constant praise we'll sing,
And raise our voices in the great amen.

Great are you, Lord, and greatly to be praised;
In all you do we see your sheer delight.
Your greatness is unsearchable but true,
Awesome in every deed of pow'r and might.

Each generation, learning of your works,
Shall tell the next of all your mighty ways,
And of the splendor of your majesty;
On these we meditate in awe and praise.

You, Lord, are just and right in all you do;
In all your dealings you are truly kind.
You come to all who call on you in truth;
These both your mercy and salvation find.

All those who fear you find their hopes fulfilled;
Hearing their cry, you save and give them joy.
You watch o'er all who come to you in love,
But every wicked one you will destroy.

Verses 1–4, 11–13

We will extol you, Lord, our God and King,
And bless your name forever without end.
With each new day your constant praise we'll sing.
And raise our voices in the great amen.

Great are you, Lord, and greatly to be praised,
Your ways unsearchable, your wisdom true.
Each generation, learning of your ways,
Shall sing unending psalms of thanks to you.

So now we sing your kingdom's glorious reign,
Telling of purpose that sustains the earth,
That all the people of this world's domain,
Shall come to know the splendor of new birth.

So bring your kingdom, bring your vict'ry, Lord,
The day your people long to see appear,
A time of peace without a need for sword,
A reign where generations have no fear.

Psalm 145 is the last of eight alphabetic, acrostic psalms, and a masterful hymn of praise that extols the Lord as God and King, focusing on all that God has done. Its emphasis is individual rather than corporate, remembering less God's acts of salvation for the nation than God's interventions and providence in personal life. The psalm is filled with some of the most memorable phrases of praise in all of scripture. "Great is the Lord, and greatly to be praised." "The Lord is gracious and merciful, slow to anger and abounding in steadfast love." "God's compassion is over all that he has made." All God's works give thanks and praise him; all the faithful shall bless him. God's kingdom is an everlasting kingdom. God's dominion endures throughout all generations. God upholds those who are falling, raises up all who are bowed down, gives food in due season, satisfies the desire of every living thing, is just in all his doings, near to all who call on him, fulfills the desires of all who fear him, hears their cries and saves them, watches over all who love him — while "all the wicked God will destroy."

Psalm 146

CM

ARLINGTON, AMAZING GRACE, AZMON

Come praise the Lord with all our lives;
Sing thanks and praise each day.
No other one is worth our hope,
For God alone can save.

How blest are those who hope in you,
Creator of all things.
You heal the sick, you feed the poor;
Your presence justice brings.

The blind find sight, the fallen hope;
You set the pris'ner free.
You give the homeless living space,
But fell the proud like trees.

Your reign, O Lord, will never end;
How can we count its days?
All generations young and old
Shall live to sing your praise.

Psalm 146 is a *Hallel* psalm (one that opens and closes with Hallelu-jah: "Praise the Lord!"). It is one of my favorites. After full-throated praise to the Lord and a promise to continue to do so all of his life, the psalmist reminds us of who alone in life is worthy of trust. "Do not put your trust in princes, in mortals, in whom there is no help. When their breath departs, they return to the earth; on that very day their plans perish." Conversely, "Blest are those whose help is the God of Jacob, whose hope is in the Lord their God." There follows a recital of all the good and marvelous things that come from God's hand — creation, faithfulness, justice for the oppressed, food to the hungry, liberty to the captive, sight to the blind, exaltation for the lowly, love for the righteous. Notice that these are characteristic the Gospels regularly celebrate in Jesus. The Lord watches over the stranger, upholds the orphan and widow, but brings the way of the wicked to ruin. In this highly politicized country, we need to remember this psalm's counsel concerning "princes," regardless of the political party they represent. The one and only source of true justice in this world is the Lord; all other systems fall short, even when we "idolize" them, and perhaps because we do!

Psalm 147

Verses 12–20
CM
ST. ANNE, ANDERSON

Now praise the Lord, all living saints;
 Sing praises that endure.
Our children God does surely bless;
 Our future is secure.

God brings us peace in midst of strife,
 Our borders to protect.
All those who trust the Lord for strength
 Need never fear neglect.

God's word runs swiftly o'er the earth,
 The seasons to command.
Spring, summer, winter, autumn all
 Display that wondrous hand.

Your life-filled Word brings order to
 The chaos of our days.
In love you claim us as your own;
 What better cause for praise?

Instruction, guidance, holy law,
 Some common names are these
For God's own rule for living life.
 What other word can please?

No other people are so graced,
 No nation is so blest,
As those who know God's living Word,
 And this one name confess.

Sing praise to God, the source of life;
Sing praise to God the Son.
Sing praise to God's life-giving pow'r,
Forever three in one.

P salm 147 is a *Hallel* psalm, beginning, as each of them does, with Hallelujah — "Praise the Lord!" The psalm celebrates God's graciousness and calls for a fitting song of praise to be sung. The reason for praise is the Lord's ability and willingness to forgive and restore, to build up and heal. The Lord builds up Jerusalem, gathers the outcasts of Israel, heals the brokenhearted, and binds up their wounds. The one who made the stars lifts up the downtrodden and casts the wicked to the ground, and delights, not in the strength of the horse or the speed of the runner, but in those who fear him and hope in his steadfast love. Now the psalmist calls on all of Jerusalem to praise the Lord, following with the parallel phrase: "Praise your God, O Zion!" God strengthens the bars of her gates and blesses the children within her. God grants her peace and fills her with the finest wheat. As God commands, the earth quickly responds, giving snow like wool. Frost is scattered like ashes. When he hurls down hail, who can stand before his cold? All of this is the creative force of God's word, melting snow, making the wind blow and the waters flow. This word God has declared to Jacob, and his statutes to Israel. God has not dealt thus with any other nation; they do not know God's ordinances. The psalm ends as it began, "Praise the Lord!"

Psalm 148

8.7.8.7 D

ODE TO JOY

Praise the Lord, sing Hallelujah;
    Shout forth praise in heaven's heights.
Angels and all heav'nly beings
    Gathered there within God's sight,
Sun and moon, all stars in heaven,
    Sing praise in celestial hymn.
Praise the Lord, sing Hallelujah;
    Bless your maker without end.

Praise the Lord, sing Hallelujah;
    Let the deeps shout forth their praise.
Fish and whales, ev'n deep-sea monsters,
    Your Creator marks your days.
Mountains, hills, fruit trees, and cedars,
    Cattle, birds, all things on land,
Fire and hail, frost, rain, and windstorm,
    Each comes forth at God's command.

Praise the Lord, sing Hallelujah,
    Kings and princes of the earth.
Young and old, both men and women,
    Praise the one who gave us birth.
Let us praise the Lord together,
    Lift our voice, and spread God's fame,
For the Lord is great and glorious;
    Let us all exalt God's name.

Praise the Lord, sing Hallelujah;
    Sing of all God's faithful ways.
We who are the Lord's beloved,
    Praise the Lord through all our days.
Strength and might unto our people,
    God, the Lord, will yet increase.
Praise the Lord, sing Hallelujah;
    Let our praises never cease.

Psalm 148 calls upon all creation — the sun, moon, stars, the highest heavens, and waters above the heavens — to shout "Hallelujah!" — "Praise the Lord!" The Lord commanded and each was created. Sea monsters and all deeps (the place of chaos), fire, hail, snow, frost, and stormy wind are not blights of nature, but actually agents that fulfill God's commands. The Lord is sovereign over all. Mountains and hills, fruit trees and cedars, wild animals and cattle, things that creep and things that fly, kings of the earth and all their people, young men and women alike, old and young together, are to praise the name of the Lord, for the Lord's name alone is to be exalted. God's glory (presence and power) is above earth and heaven. Finally, all are to shout "Hallelujah" because the Lord has "raised up a horn for his people" (the horn being a symbol of deliverance and strength that is often used to speak of Israel's kings). But now, the dignity, honor, and praise due the king are given not to the king, but to the people of Israel who are close to the Lord. Hallelujah!

Psalm 149

CMD

ELLACOMBE

O praise the Lord; sing unto God
    A new and joyful song.
Assembled as God's holy ones,
    Sing praise with voices strong.
Be glad, for God has made us all;
    Rejoice, our Lord is King.
With dancing, drums, with organ strong,
    God's praises let us sing.

The Lord takes pleasure in our lives,
    To give us victory.
All those who live in humble trust
    Will triumph and be free.
Let thankful songs of joy and praise
    Come from us in our ease.
This peace is God's own gift to all
    Who in the Lord believe.

In times of war, in times of strife,
    Our songs shall bless the Lord.
Lest victory and all its fame
    Be seen as our reward.
O praise the Lord, sing with full strength
    A new and joyful song.
Assembled as God's holy ones,
    Sing praise with voices strong.

P salm 149 is another "Hallelujah" psalm that calls on the assembly to "sing to the Lord a new song." Employing Hebrew parallelisms, the psalm calls on Israel to be glad in its Maker, while the children of Zion are to rejoice in God their King, making melody with tambourine and lyre, and praising him with dancing. The Lord takes pleasure in his people, adorning the humble with victory. Let the high praises of God be in their throats as the two-edged battle sword is in their hands, executing God's vengeance against their enemies, binding the defeated king in fetters and his nobles in chains. This is less the people's doing than judgment decreed by the Lord. It is glory for all of God's faithful and ends as it begins with a Hallelujah — "praise the Lord!"

Psalm 150

6.6.6.6.4.8.4
DARWELL'S 148TH

To you, our Holy God,
    We bring our praises strong.
We call on all to laud
    And sing your joyful song.
Sing praise to God,
Who is the sovereign of all things.
    O praise the Lord!

You rule with might and strength,
    Above the firmament.
We call on all in heav'n
    And earth to give assent.
Sing praise to God,
Who is the sovereign of all things.
    O praise the Lord!

We sing of pow'r and strength,
    Transcending time and space.
With trumpet, flute, with reed
    And pipe engulf this place
To offer praise
To God, the sovereign of all things.
    O praise the Lord!

Now make the drums beat strong,
    To drive our dancing feet.
Bells, cymbals, join our song
    With loud percussive beat.
Ring praise to God,
Who is the sovereign of all things.
    O praise the Lord!

Let every living thing
Join in this song of praise.
All creatures join and sing;
Praise God through all your days.
Sing praise to God,
Who is the sovereign of all things.
O praise the Lord!

Psalm 150 brings the Psalter to a proper conclusion with a hymn of praise calling upon everything and everyone to shout "Hallelujah!" — Praise the Lord! The hymn begins praising God within God's heavenly sanctuary above the firmament and then moves to the firmament itself. Praise begins simply as the acclaim that befits God as God. Only then does it move to praising God for his mighty deeds and surpassing greatness as the source and sustainer of all that is. Musical instruments and dance are called upon to join and take up their part in worship as each is reminded that their first and foremost purpose is simply to praise the Lord. Finally, everything that breathes is called to praise the Lord. And then, fitting to the whole collection, there is one last "Hallelujah!"

CANTICLES

Song of Hannah (1 Samuel 2:1–10)

7.6.7.6. D
ES FLOG EIN KLEINS WALDVÖGELEIN

My heart exults in you, Lord;
  In you my strength grows strong.
My mouth mocks my opponents,
  In triumph o'er their wrong.
There is no one like you, Lord,
  So holy and so good,
No rock secure or constant
  As you, O Lord, my God.

Proud talk and haughty slander
  Must stop – not be let loose.
God knows all thoughts and motives,
  And weighs all things in truth.
The strong men's bows are broken;
  The feeble grow in strength.
The rich for bread go begging;
  The hungry find relief.

The Lord brings down and lifts up,
  Cuts down and brings to life.
The Lord exalts and humbles,
  Makes rich and poor alike.
God lifts the poor and downcast,
  The needy from their plight,
And gives them seats of honor
  Midst royals and their like.

The pillars of creation
  Were made by God alone,
Who set the world upon them
  To make this earth our home.

The Lord guards all the faithful,
  But cuts the wicked down.
Exalt, Lord, your anointed,
  With strength and great renown.

The barren Hannah offers a prayer of thanksgiving upon learning that God is taking away her barrenness and giving her a son who will become the prophet Samuel. Scholars think that this is a national hymn of thanksgiving, developed much later, but inserted here by the editors of 1 Samuel, because it is such an apt description of the Lord's concern for those oppressed and in trouble. The Lord is named "Holy One," "Rock." He is the one who breaks the bows of the mighty but girds the feeble with strength. In a series of divine reversals, those who had abundance now must hire themselves out for a living, while the poor now have in abundance. All of this is the work of the Lord, who comes to the help of all in need. The theme of barrenness — a source of great personal shame for a woman in that culture — is addressed: "the barren has borne seven, but she who has many children is forlorn." The text is a classic expression of what is called Deuteronomic theology, the belief that God rewards the righteous and punishes the wicked, celebrating and giving thanks for God's deliverance from oppression in many forms. It is this poem that lies behind Mary's song of thanksgiving known as the *Magnificat,* which she sings upon learning that she is to bear Jesus (Luke 1:46–55).

Isaiah 12:2–6

9.8.9.8 D

RENDEZ À DIEU *(preferred tune)*, LES COMMANDEMENTS DE DIEU

Surely the Lord is my salvation;
Trust God and do not be afraid.
Lord God, you are my consolation,
True source of strength, my constant aid.
Joyful, we drink of your salvation,
A cup of trust that drives out fear.
Gladly we say to every nation:
"Great is our Lord who's always near."

Sing praise to God, whose works are glorious;
Through all the earth let this be known.
Shout loud, and sing for joy, O Zion;
Great is the Holy One alone.
Call on God's name in adoration;
Give thanks in every thought and deed.
Shout loud, and sing for joy, O Zion:
"Great is the Lord, our God, indeed!"

Isaiah has just announced the restoration of Israel by the messianic shoot that will come forth out of the stump of Jesse. In response, it appears that editors have inserted this five-verse psalm of praise, introduced by a verse that acknowledges that, though the Lord was angry, God has turned that anger away and brought comfort. Thus, "Surely God is my salvation." Notice how personal this song is; it is not a communal word of thanksgiving: "*I* will trust . . . , the Lord is *my* strength and *my* might, he has become *my* salvation." Then, is it God or is it the psalmist speaking a word of additional promise: "You will draw water from the wells of salvation"? The response that follows suggests that it is the Lord speaking, and so the psalmist responds, calling for everyone to sing praises to the Lord, and to let his glorious deeds be known throughout the earth. "Give thanks to the Lord, call on his name; make known his deeds among the nations — proclaim that his name is exalted." This song of praise concludes by calling on "royal Zion" to shout aloud and sing, for "great in your midst is the Holy One of Israel."

Isaiah 58:1–12

7.6.7.6 D

NYLAND, WIE LIEBLICH IST DER MAIEN

Shout out, sound as a ram's horn.
    Declare; do not hold back.
Proclaim my people's failure,
    Their faithlessness attack.
Day after day they seek me,
    As if they knew my ways,
And ask for righteous judgments
    As payment for their praise.

"Why do we fast?" they ask me,
    "And yet, you do not see.
Why bow and scrape before you?
    No notice will there be!"
You fast for your own purpose,
    To fill your own desire.
Is this the fast I ask for,
    The worship I admire?

The fast that I desire
    Frees people from their yokes,
Undoing their oppression,
    Removing all that chokes.
It shares bread with the hungry,
    Receives the homeless in.
It gives the naked clothing,
    And hides not from one's kin.

Such fasting I will honor,
    Such worship I reward,
And like the light at morning,
    Breaks forth to bless the Lord,

Then shall your healing spring up,
  And vindication rise,
And when you call I'll answer,
  I'll hearken to your cries.

Remove the yoke among you,
  The pointing finger too.
Give food unto the hungry,
  The suffering's pains undo.
Then light shall rise in darkness,
  Your gloom be like noonday.
Your name will be "repairer,"
  And I will bless your way.

The Jews had returned from Babylonian exile with a new sense of scrupulosity concerning matters of worship, fasting, and the like. But, like many overtly religious people over the centuries, though meticulous about the form, they were missing the point of it all, overlooking the more fundamental issues in life: care for those around them in need. The newly returned exiles had experienced more hardship than Isaiah had foretold, and they are now complaining to the Lord, saying, "Why do we fast, but you do not see? Why do we humble ourselves, but you do not notice?" What's the use of being religious if it does not pay off good dividends? Consequently, this oracle from the Lord is leveled against the people to call them to judgment and, in the process, distinguish between worship that is authentic and worship that is merely an attempted *quid pro quo* — a means of getting what one wants from the Lord. The charges against the people are direct: they serve their own interests on fast days, not unlike the Christian whose Lenten fast is designed more to lose weight than to draw the person into a more intimate and dependent relationship with God. More, they continue to oppress their workers. And, when they fast, it is not long before they are quarreling and fighting with one another. None of this will make their voice heard by the Lord. Now true fasting and penance are defined. Fasting is not deprivation of this or that form of food or drink, or covering oneself in sackcloth and ashes. The fast acceptable to the Lord is a fast of justice: to loosen the bonds of injustice, undo the thongs of the yoke, let the oppressed go free, and break every yoke that binds and weighs people down. But it is even more basic than that. It has to do with feeding the hungry, clothing the naked, housing the homeless, and responding to the needs of one's extended family, rather than looking the other way. This is the worship the Lord seeks: attending to the needs of the afflicted and doing something about them beyond criticizing or blaming them for their own circumstances, as too often happens in our culture. God promises that when we begin to care for those among us in need, God will guide us continually, satisfy our needs, and make us strong, like a watered garden. The ancient ruins of Jerusalem shall be rebuilt, raising up the foundations of the city laid by many generations, repairing the breaches in the city's walls, and restoring its streets. The oracle ends by pressing the issue of sabbath observance. This seems not to have been an issue in Babylon, but it has become one in the returned community. The sabbath is not a day for work or for pursuing one's own interests or personal affairs, not to mention one's hobbies! It is a day holy to the Lord, to be kept holy and to be used to honor the Lord. When the people do that and take delight in the day and its purposes, the Lord will see to it that they "ride upon the heights of the earth." God will feed them with the heritage of their ancestor Jacob.

Lamentations 3:19–26

CMD

RESIGNATION, SEACHRIST, MOSHIER

My misery and homelessness
    Are ever on my mind,
As wormwood in its bitterness,
    As gall in all its brine.
The thought of my life's emptiness
    Is much too much to know.
My soul remembers in its grief,
    Recalls and is bowed low.

But this one thing I call to mind,
    Herein my hope defend:
Your steadfast love, O Lord, is true;
    Its riches never end.
Your mercies come and never cease;
    Each morning they are new.
Your faithfulness is great, indeed,
    To all who wait on you.

You are my portion, Lord, my God;
    In you, no hope is vain.
You show your goodness and your love
    To those who seek your name.
All those who wait on you in trust,
    Your true salvation find.
My heart awaits you quietly,
    As this I call to mind.

In Lamentations chapter 2, the focus is upon the women of Zion and their suffering. Here in chapter 3 the focus is upon a man (though the NRSV's commitment to inclusive language obscures the fact that this is a man speaking). Is the man Jeremiah, speaking out of his own suffering? Or another prophet, or the king? Or is this man simply the personification of the entire community, as were the women in the lament in the previous chapter? This is God's wrath at work; it is the Lord who has driven the man into darkness without any light and has turned the divine hand against him, again and again — all day long! The language is bitter complaint about affliction and homelessness — it is wormwood and gall! His soul can think of no other thing and is bowed down within him. But this he calls to mind, and herein he finds hope, and now, like so many of the laments in the psalms, the poet focuses upon the steadfast love of the Lord — it never ceases, its mercies never end. He affirms, "Great is [God's] faithfulness" — words that formed the foundation of the famous hymn, "Great Is Thy Faithfulness." Confessing that the Lord is his portion, the poet finds hope in God. What follows is a confession of the goodness of the Lord for those who wait on him and his salvation. More, it is good to bear the yoke of burden in one's youth, to sit alone in silence, when that silence is imposed by the Lord, to put one's mouth to the dust in penance, and to give one's cheek to those who smite and insult him (an image that will be incorporated into the passion narrative). And why? Because the Lord will not reject forever. Although the Lord causes grief, he also has compassion, according to the abundance of his steadfast love. The Lord does not willingly afflict or grieve anyone. The message to a lamenting Jerusalem is clear, just as it is clear to any today who suffer, justly or unjustly: wait on the Lord, and he will come with salvation.

Song of Mary (Luke 1:47–55)

CMD

SHEPHERD'S PIPES

I magnify you, Lord, my God;
    In you I do rejoice.
In favor you have looked on me,
    My lowliness your choice.
All generations now shall say
    "How blest is Mary's name!"
How holy is your name, O Lord;
    You put away my shame.

Your mercy is for all who fear
    Your name in every way.
You scatter both the proud and vain;
    Their ways you put away.
The mighty you dethrone and shame;
    You lift the lowly up.
The rich are empty, sent away;
    The hungry richly sup.

Your servant Isr'el you have helped,
    Your mercy ever sure.
To Abraham and all his seed
    Your promises endure.
Come, magnify the Lord with me;
    In this let us rejoice:
God's tender mercy shall not fail.
    Give thanks; lift up your voice!

Upon learning that she is pregnant, Mary withdraws to the hill country to live with her older cousin Elizabeth and her husband Zechariah, only to find that Elizabeth, who has been barren, is now in the sixth month of her own pregnancy. When the two cousins meet, the babe (who will be John the Baptist) leaps in Elizabeth's womb, which she interprets as his welcome greeting. And so Elizabeth asks, "How is it that the mother of my Lord comes to me?" — thereby affirming again what the angel had said to Mary. Elizabeth then blesses Mary for believing what has been promised to her by Gabriel. Mary's response of humility and thanksgiving is both a masterpiece of commentary upon her role and life in the gospel story and a magnificent adaptation of the song of Hannah (1 Sam. 2:1–10), who breaks into thanksgiving upon learning that her barrenness has been taken away by the Lord. There the theme of divine reversals first finds its voice; but here, it comes to fullness in Mary's song: "The Mighty One has done great things for me, and holy is his name." Song, after all, has been the historic response to God's intervention on behalf of God's people (Exod. 15:1–18, 20–21; Judg. 5:1–31), for this is not just about Mary but about Mary's people as well. The Lord's mercy is for all who fear him, from generation to generation. But more than even that, this is the fulfillment of help to the Lord's servant Israel, a promise made long ago to the nation's ancestors Abraham and Sarah.

Song of Zechariah (Luke 1:68–79)

6.6.8.4 D

LEONI

How blest are you, O Lord,
    The God of Israel,
In favor you have looked on us,
    Redeeming still.
As prophets did foretell,
    From David's house you've raised
A voice to save us from our foes.
    His name be praised!

In him you have shown forth
    Your promises of old,
The oath you swore to Abraham,
    To us foretold.
That safe from every foe,
    And armed with acts of nerve,
In holiness and righteousness,
    We would you serve.

This promised child shall be
    Your prophet, O Most High.
To speak your word, make straight your path,
    And call us nigh;
To teach salvation's ways,
    And call us back again,
And by your tender mercies still
    Forgive our sin.

The mercy of our God
    Has dawned now from on high,
To give us light 'mid shades of death;
    On it rely.

Your tender ways, O Lord,
 For us will never cease,
  To guide our feet into the way
   Of your true peace.

The aged priest Zechariah had been struck speechless because he failed to believe God's promise that he and his barren wife Elizabeth would have a son. The son is born, and when the boy is to be given a name (the wrong one, by the way) Zechariah's tongue is suddenly loosened, and he sings a psalm of thanksgiving on the birth of his son John the Baptist, a song the church knows as the *Benedictus*. It falls in three parts. The first stanza blesses God for having looked favorably on his people Israel and redeemed them. The act of redemption is spoken of in the past tense, because it has already begun to unfold in the birth of his son. God has raised up a mighty savior for the house of David in the babe coming to birth in his wife's cousin, Mary. All of this is God acting to fulfill the ancient promise made to Abraham and Sarah, to bring forth from them a covenant people who might worship and serve God without fear, and do so in holiness and righteousness all their days. The hymn moves into its second stanza as Zechariah lifts his son into his arms to prophesy concerning him. John is to be the prophet of the Most High who will prepare the way for the Son of the Most High, giving the knowledge of salvation to the people — the forgiveness of sins. Stanza three tells us that all of this is the result of the tender mercies of our God. The "dawn" breaking from on high is the promised Messiah, who comes to give light to those sitting in darkness and the shadow of death. His way is the way of peace.

Song of Simeon (Luke 2:29–32)

9.8.8.9
RANDOLF *(preferred tune)*

Lord, now let your servants go in peace,
    For our eyes see your salvation,
    Laud to Isr'el, light of nations.
Lord, now let your servants go in peace.

Lord, now give to us a night of rest.
    As the darkness falls around us,
    Keep us safe; let none confound us.
Lord, now give to us a night of rest.

Lord, now give to us your perfect peace.
    Keep us true and your own people,
    That in deed and witness faithful,
We, your servants, may go forth in peace.

6.6.7 D
To be sung to NUNC DIMITTIS *(Louis Bourgeois, 1551)*

Lord, send us forth in peace
    According to your Word.
For we have seen Christ present,
    Promised from long ago,
Light to make known your will,
    And bring your people glory.

Give us your grace and peace,
    And mercy in our rest,

Preserve us in your gospel
As we go forth from here.
That both in word and deed
Christ may be known within us.

L eviticus 12 designated all mothers of newborn boys as unclean for thirty-three days, at which time the mother was to come to the temple to offer a sacrifice for purification; that would enable her to enter the full life of the community again. In Mary and Joseph's case, the sacrifice is a pair of turtledoves or two young pigeons — the sacrifice prescribed for the poor. When the thirty-three days are past, Mary, Joseph, and their newborn boy go to Jerusalem to offer the sacrifice. There, they encounter an old man named Simeon, who we are told was "righteous and devout, looking forward to the consolation of Israel, and the Holy Spirit rested on him." The Spirit had revealed to Simeon that he would not die before he had seen the Lord's Messiah. And so, as Mary and Joseph make their way to the temple, the Spirit also leads Simeon there; and, when they meet, Simeon takes the child in his arms and sings a song of praise that the church has ever after known as the *Nunc dimittis*. Simeon recognizes that, in the fulfillment of this promise, he is being "dismissed in peace," for he has seen the Lord's salvation, "a light for revelation to the Gentiles and for the glory of God's people, Israel."